WRITING ABOUT

SUCCESSFUL WRITING

WRITING ABOUT TRAVEL

How to research, write and sell
travel guides and articles

Brian & Eileen Anderson

How To Books

Cartoons by Mike Flanagan

British Library Cataloguing in Publication Data
A catalogue record for this book is available from the British Library.

© Copyright 1998 by Brian & Eileen Anderson.

First published in 1998 by How To Books Ltd, 3 Newtec Place,
Magdalen Road, Oxford OX4 1RE, United Kingdom.
Tel: (01865) 793806. Fax: (01865) 248780.

Note: The material contained in this book is set out in good faith for
general guidance and no liability can be accepted for loss or expense
incurred as a result of relying in particular circumstances on statements made
in this book. The law and regulations are complex and liable to change, and
readers should check the current position with the relevant authorities before
making personal arrangements.

Produced for How To Books by Deer Park Productions.
Typeset by PDQ Typesetting, Stoke-on-Trent, Staffs.
Printed and bound by Cromwell Press, Trowbridge, Wiltshire.

Contents

List of Illustrations

Foreword

Merely buying this book sets you apart from most people who toy with the idea of becoming a travel writer. They think it is money for old rope, needing no skill other than how to cope with jet lag and spell bougainvillaea, and that anybody who has ever been on holiday can write about it. Oh, and they were 'good at essays' at school anyway.

Being good at essays is no drawback, but self-discipline is also vital and most people don't have it to the necessary degree. The discipline to work while all around you are taking it easy (because they are on holiday and you are not). The discipline to meet deadlines when you are back at your domestic base (because if you let somebody down once that person will never use your work again).

This book will take you through the nuts and bolts of getting started, researching, selling your ideas, scheduling work trips and so on. And all that is just for starters. Because then comes the vital business of developing a distinctive writing style and selling yourself to potential employers. That you have to learn for yourself.

Oh, and one other thing. When you have finally made it – after years of hard slog – and are working at full stretch with no time to take a break, be prepared for all those people who will say: 'Life's one long holiday to you.' Smile pleasantly and let them go on believing it, because you'll never get them to change their minds.

John Carter

Preface

Travel writing is seen with some justification as an enviable profession. Like any other job, it has its pressures and rewards, its good times and its bad times. Every travel writer can relate horror stories of travelling, delays, hardship and tiring journeys. The fun side is very obvious; visiting exotic places, experiencing quality hotels and leaving footprints in the sand of the world's most beautiful beaches.

Writers rarely talk about the real benefits, the deep personal enrichment from experiencing and writing about other cultures. Something of yourself goes into every piece of written work. The knowledge that readers find pleasure in an article is the icing on the cake for the writer. It simply reinforces the pleasure and satisfaction already experienced.

New writers are constantly entering the profession. Some, like John Carter, rise to become stars of television travel programmes. Not everybody can rise to the top but many travel writers enjoy a fruitful and varied career. There is no one particular way to get started. For us it is a second career and, if you follow the fortunes of Mike and Susan in the case studies, they loosely mirror our own entry into the world of travel writing.

People always ask us the secret of getting started but they rarely like the answer. It is simple – solid groundwork, constant application and dedicated professionalism from the outset. These themes have been pursued relentlessly through this book. They worked for us and they will work for you. Good luck!

Brian and Eileen Anderson

1
Getting Started

A cool assessment of your own potential is a valuable exercise anytime in a career. It is an essential exercise when starting out in a new direction for a number of important reasons:

- To ensure your personal skills are at least a broad match with the job requirements. Unless skills match hope and ambition there is nothing but disappointment in store.

- To identify your own strengths and to make sure these are fully utilised from the beginning.

- To identify your own weaknesses. Acknowledging weaknesses is the first step towards improving them. You can avoid work areas in the beginning which will instantly expose them. For example, if your photography is not up to scratch, avoid writing work which is picture oriented until your camera skills have improved sufficiently.

LOOKING AT JOB REQUIREMENTS

The market for travel writers, discussed more fully in Chapter 3, has some complexity which places different demands on its contributors. Nevertheless, good writing skills remain the prime requirement. As if writing skills are not enough, the industry is increasingly choosing to work with authors who can also take good pictures.

Writing skills
As long as you can organise your thoughts and express them clearly in words you have reached the starting point. Writing skills, like anything else, can be improved and will improve with constant practice. The more you write, the easier it becomes and your aim

should be to write something every day even if it is only a diary. Just as important is the way you write or your style.

Style

Look up 'style' in a dictionary and you will probably find around twenty definitions. It is a word which comes into its own when more precise terms fail. In writing it is the manner in which a writer expresses ideas in words. Just as you have a style in speech, you also have a style in writing. Like other aspects of writing, it will develop and blossom with practice. In time you will learn to make adjustments to your style to meet the various market demands (see Chapter 3).

Photography

Magazines rely heavily on colour pictures; newspapers and guide-books are moving in the same direction. Commercial photographic libraries exist to keep the industry supplied with suitable photographs and the system works well within limitations. It is a time-consuming process for a publisher to hunt around the libraries looking for a specific photograph. The ideal solution for a publisher is to use an author who can supply quality photographs to illustrate the submitted article. It saves the publisher time and money and results in a finished article where the pictures truly support the words.

With improvements in all aspects of photography in recent years, in cameras, lenses and film, any well-equipped person with a basic understanding can take quality pictures. The following chapter pursues this theme in more detail.

CHECKING PERSONAL SKILLS

Writing is only one side of the coin. The other side relates to working out in the field gathering information. Both aspects of a travel writer's job require dedication but they are very different in skill requirements. Leaving the office to go out on location, which may be anything from your local airport to a trip to China, is seen as the glamorous part of the work which attracts many to the industry. Do not be misled. This is often the most taxing part of the work upon which the success of the article depends. Take a look at some of the skills which are brought into play throughout a project.

Collecting information

More than likely, this will require travelling out to visit the area or site which is to be the subject of the piece. Some prior reading will help in the appreciation and may be absolutely essential in some cases. If the article or book is about ancient Ephesus in Turkey, for example, it could not be written without a good historical background. Similarly, for important churches and cathedrals, some architectural knowledge would be expected. Knowledge is there to be learnt and it can all be acquired with time and effort. Combine this learning with curiosity, appreciation, an eye for detail and good record keeping and this part of the job profile starts to take shape.

Being back in the office

This is where organisation and self-discipline take over. Writing takes time and there are usually deadlines to meet. Deadlines are not frivolous impositions laid on to journalists. They are important stages in a publisher's need to get the project to the printing stage on schedule. Failure to meet targets on the journalist's part usually means looking elsewhere for future work.

If you are working from home, good organisation is especially important. You will need to set aside an area with a space for working and space for storage. Eventually, as the work grows, so will the office chores. There will be letters, leaflets and brochures to file, people to contact and schedules to plan.

Try your hand at the self-assessment test shown in Figure 1. It assumes basic writing skills and concentrates on the other qualities needed to make a successful travel writer. With a maximum of 230, a score of:

- 180 or more means you are well on your way

- between 140 and 180 leaves you with some work to do

- less than 140 means it is time to question your motivation.

LOOKING AT SPECIAL INTERESTS

Instead of heading directly into the mainstream of travel writing, it is sometimes easier to enter at the periphery. Holidaymakers do more these days than simply lying on the beach. They take part in all sorts of activities like walking in the countryside, playing golf, sailing and many other pastimes. This sector of the market has been growing steadily over the past few years and will probably continue to grow. There are plenty of work opportunities here and anyone with a specialised knowledge starts with an advantage over the

Are you:	Yes	Moderately	No
a good traveller	15	10	0
brimming with enthusiasm	15	10	0
curious	20	15	0
persistent	20	10	0
self-disciplined	20	10	0
meticulous	20	5	0
a collector	10	5	0
a good communicator	15	5	0
keen on detail	20	10	0
perceptive	15	10	0
willing to learn	20	10	0
good at research	20	10	0
a good photographer?	20	10	0

Fig. 1. Self-assessment test.

average travel writer.

Although by no means exhaustive, this list highlights activities which could easily feature in travel articles or be the subject of a guidebook:

- walking
- fishing
- sailing
- water sports
- food and wine
- golf
- railways
- gardening
- drawing and painting.

Once a foothold has been gained in a specialist area then options start to open up. If plenty of work is forthcoming then it might be wise to become entrenched and establish a name. Having collected a list of publications to add to your CV, it is easier to move into the area of general travel.

BEING PROFESSIONAL

Only the highest quality work is going to succeed in this competitive field. The aim at the outset must be for high standards both in content and presentation. Presentation is especially important. When a finished piece of work drops on an editor's desk, whether speculative or commissioned, the appearance of the work tells the editor volumes about the author. If it is hand-written then there is a chance that it will never reach the top of the slush pile. Handwriting is not as quickly read as a neatly typed piece of work, so busy editors tend to push them aside. Very often they get returned with a rejection slip without even being opened.

Exploring the tools of the trade

Work needs to be finished either in type or on a word processor. A word processor is almost essential for book writing since the publisher may require submission on a disk as well as printed copy. It does not matter which process is used for articles as long as the finished piece looks professional.

Typewriters

Good typewriters can be acquired relatively cheaply these days and there are some electronic models which carry out a few word processing functions. Several lines of type appear on a small screen so they can be checked for spelling before printing. They work extremely well, produce a good finished product but lack so many advantages of a word processor. The biggest disadvantage is the time factor. If you are not satisfied with the completed article and wish to rework the piece, it may mean typing it all again.

Word processors

The world of computers is full of high tech jargon with a continual emphasis on speed and power. Machine specifications improve almost every month and the pressure is to buy bigger and better. None of that matters at all if the machine is to be used mainly for word processing. Machines on sale in the 1980s without the benefit of hard disks and big memories coped perfectly well with the task of writing articles and books. The most basic of machines and simplest of word processing programmes will produce entirely satisfactory work.

Printers

There is a huge selection on the market but there is no need to go to any great expense. Many of these print in colour but, unless you have other applications in mind, it is better to buy a simple black and white machine. Dot matrix printers, one of the earliest kinds, are still available but the cheaper ones tend to be noisy. Better still are the inkjet printers which are fairly silent in operation and give excellent results. The inks used are not always waterproof so they are not so good for printing addresses on envelopes. Laser printers give the best quality and can be obtained at around the same price as an inkjet printer.

Using a word processor

As far as computing goes, word processing is a relatively simple task. Many people teach themselves but there are various courses of instruction available. It takes only a few lessons to gain a basic proficiency. Most publishers require nothing elaborate, all they want is words on paper just as if they had been typed.

New users especially like to compose their work on paper before transferring it to the computer, but others prefer to compose directly on the screen, watching the words appear as they are typed. It matters little which approach is used although typing speed is more important with the former approach. When composing at the screen, thinking time usually determines rate of progress so you can get by easily with one finger typing.

A word processor comes into its own when you start to tidy up your work. The spell-checker will quickly pick up wrong spellings and these can be easily corrected. Words or blocks of text can be moved around at will, text can be cut out at the stroke of a key and new text added anywhere in the document. When all is finished, the line spacing can be adjusted to whatever the editor requires, usually double spacing, and another button will send everything to the printer. Minutes later a pristine document will be ready for dispatch.

Storage is another advantage gained from a word processor. All your work, finished articles, part worked pieces, and letters can be stored electronically either on the hard disk of your computer or on floppy disk. Retrieval is much simpler and it saves storing mountains of paper. It is sensible always to store everything important in duplicate on separate disks.

SETTING UP AS A FREELANCE

It is all about perception and it is important to appear professional from the moment of starting out as a travel writer. There are one or two things to do initially which will help to create the right image.

Looking professional

Letterhead
A business style letterhead for your correspondence is important. This is easy to organise and store on a word processor. It can be introduced at the top of every letter you write. If you are short on design ideas, just study some of the business letters which arrive on your own doormat. Figure 2 shows a straightforward design which might be used.

A. N. Other
10 Book Street, Storyville, Wordshire XXXX XXX
Tel & Fax: xxxx xxx xxx

Fig. 2. Typical letterhead.

There is scope for playing around with fonts, point size and layout. For those connected to the Internet, do not forget to add your e-mail address. Once you have had a few articles or a travel book published, you will be justified in incorporating 'Freelance Travel Writer' into the heading.

Those without a word processor will need to follow the traditional route and have a batch of personal letterheads printed.

Business cards
For a freelance in any form of business, personal contacts are particularly important. If you visit a travel show and engage in conversation with staff from a tourist office, for example, handing over a business card starts to bind a relationship. If you express particular interest in their country you might find that they start to send you press releases. This can be particularly helpful, not just by keeping you in the picture, but in helping to formulate ideas for articles.

Fax facilities

This is by no means top of the start-up list but it will be useful as work builds up. Journalism always seems to be an industry in a hurry. Whenever your work is being edited, the editor will be in touch asking for adjustments or corrections to your piece. Time-scales can be quite short, hours rather than days. This is when the faxes fly backward and forward and the machine starts to earn its keep. Modern computers are equipped with fax facilities but electronic transfer by e-mail is gaining wider acceptance.

Bookkeeping

Like any small business, you will need to keep records. When you are ready to send out work or proposals for work, it is important to log the details. Log the date sent, the publisher and the response. Keeping accounts is a good discipline and will become necessary if the business grows. Keep records of all purchases with receipts and note all legitimate expenditure.

CHECKLIST

- Assess your own qualities against the job requirements.

- Decide if a special interest offers opportunities for work.

- Plan how to organise and equip an office.

- Consider how you will present a clean and professional manuscript.

CASE STUDIES

Caroline needs a challenge

Caroline is in her mid-30s and has chosen to take a break from her professional career in management to take care of her two young children until they are both at school. Mark is at school full time while Sally attends day care three mornings a week. She lives with her husband Tom on the borders of Devon and Cornwall. With two years before she can contemplate a return to work, Caroline feels the need for a stimulating project which she can run from home in her own time and is attracted by the idea of writing travel articles. She is no stranger to office work and is fully competent on a word processor. They have a family computer at home which she will use.

Mike and Susan take early retirement

At the age of 50, Mike took early retirement from his position as Research Chemist and within a year Susan left her job as an English teacher for the same reason. They see early retirement as an exciting opportunity to develop a new career, this time working together and for themselves. Both of them love travel and Mike is already a good photographer, so they feel that writing travel guides offers the sort of challenge they are looking for and would be the ideal vehicle for their combined skills.

Both Mike and Susan are familiar with computers and word processing and already have a suitable machine at home. They do not have a fax machine but realise it may bring advantages and have budgeted to acquire one if it becomes necessary.

Rob looks for a career in travel journalism

Since university, Rob has taken a year out to backpack around Asia. While he was there, he managed to pick up some work with an adventure holiday company leading trekking and overland travel tours. He stayed away much longer than he originally planned but now he is back home and needs to start his career. The yearning for travel is still with him so he has enrolled for a course on journalism and plans to become a travel writer.

At the moment he is living at home with his parents and the idea of a static office does not fit his plans. Instead he plans to invest in a notebook-size computer with communication facilities which he can take on his travels. He intends to make it his complete office, not just for writing, but for storing and maintaining records.

2
Taking Pictures

There is a huge market for pictures in the world of publishing. Almost every article on travel is accompanied by at least one photograph and a travel guide may be illustrated with more than a hundred.

INCREASING WORK OPPORTUNITIES

Usually, a writer plays a leading role in writing the words of a feature or book while the photographer plays a supporting role in providing photographs. It is an enormous advantage if a writer can do both, in securing work and increasing income.

Understanding budgets

Budgets usually dictate how the photographs are obtained for a particular piece.

High budgets

When a project is backed by a large budget, the publisher will commission a photographer to accompany the author. This happens with top magazines where highest picture quality is required. If the author happens to be a particularly good photographer then both commissions may be awarded which makes a job very lucrative.

Normal budgets

For the great majority of magazines and books, budgets are much tighter. Obtaining photographs is much more of a problem in these circumstances. It may mean the editor has to spend time in scouting around the various picture agencies to find illustrations which will support a particular article and pay a fee to use them. On the other hand, if an author can provide photographs fit for publication, chances of obtaining work are greatly increased. Photographs surplus to the immediate project may also be saleable and earnings are considerably increased.

Low budgets
Too many projects are launched on a limited budget, and this is often true of guidebooks, where the author has a contractual obligation to provide photographs without the provision of an extra fee. An author would be expected to submit a small portfolio of pictures before such a contract was awarded. Work such as this is often turned down by those established in the industry as not lucrative enough. On the other hand, it provides opportunities for aspiring travel writers to get published and get started.

DECIDING ON A SUITABLE CAMERA

Before looking at camera requirements, it is important to understand two things:

1. The industry largely uses slide films for reproducing quality colour pictures. Print films are used to produce brochures and similar where quality is less important.

2. 35mm format is now widely acceptable for quality reproduction. Professionals mostly use larger formats but these cameras are expensive and the equipment heavy.

Looking at compact cameras
There has been a huge growth in 35mm compact cameras over the past few years and they have grown in sophistication. Whilst they are excellent for taking print films, they handle slide films less well. Part of this lies in the nature of these two types of film. Print film has considerable exposure latitude. A hopelessly wrong exposure can still yield an acceptable print. Slide film demands an almost perfect exposure. Exposure errors lead to a slide which is either too dark or too light and fit only for the bin. Generally, metering systems on compact cameras are not accurate enough to handle slide films well under a wide range of lighting conditions.

A further disadvantage is that the lens is fixed and cannot be substituted which limits the scope and usefulness of this type of camera. Compacts are not the best choice nor are the APS (Advanced Photographic System) cameras which have evolved and which use a smaller film area.

Having said that compact cameras are not the best choice, quite a lot of journalists do use them for taking colour prints. Many of them succeed in having their pictures published in newspapers and magazines in support of their own articles. An aspiring journalist must always aim for the highest standards. In some respects, double standards apply. A newcomer must be even more professional in all respects to oust a regular contributor and that includes photographic skills.

Using 35mm SLR cameras

SLR simply means single lens reflex. Whereas compact cameras have two lenses on the front, one for the viewfinder and one for taking the photograph, an SLR has just one. The viewfinder looks through the same lens used for taking the photograph. What you see is more or less what you take, so that pictures can be framed with much greater accuracy. State of the art cameras might sound complicated but they are extremely easy to use. Anyone with an eye for a picture can start to take pictures fit for publication with just a little practice.

There are many inbuilt features which are making life easier for photographers.

Autofocus

A touch of the button and the scene leaps into focus. The system has improved steadily since it was introduced. It works quickly and accurately and can, on some cameras, be used to track moving objects.

Metering

Modern cameras have multizone metering. This means that computers in the camera divide the scene about to be taken into a number of areas, usually about six or eight. Some of these will be bright sky areas and some will be darker foreground regions. The inbuilt computers instantly balance the effect of the different areas to determine an accurate exposure in most cases. There are some circumstances, easily recognised, where even this fails but this is discussed later.

Lenses

Lenses are interchangeable on SLR cameras. It takes only a moment or two to change one for another and it can be done while the film is in the camera. With such a wide range of high quality lenses available, it adds considerable versatility. Some cameras are still purchased with a standard 50mm lens, the lens regarded as giving the most normal view of a scene, but more and more are sold with a zoom lens.

The popular zooms are usually from 35 to 80mm, a particularly useful range for picture composition. A view of the scene can be widened or narrowed just by sliding the lens in or out. This size of zoom covers a great majority of picture situations but there are occasions when a wide angle down to 24mm might be appropriate or a telephoto lens up to 200 or 300mm.

There are zoom lenses of all sizes available but a useful combination would be a 24–50mm with a 35–80mm and a 70–200m. This would meet most picture-taking requirements for travel photography.

CHOOSING FILM

There is a good range of quality slide film available on the market from the various manufacturers. They vary a little in colour balance and sharpness and most brands have their followers. Professional photographers in particular are concerned about colour saturation, sharpness and how well transparencies convert into print. Not surprisingly, two of the largest manufacturers lead the way, Fuji and Kodak. Before considering films in more detail, film speed needs some discussion.

Understanding film speed

A fast film, indicated by a higher number, *eg* 400ASA, requires less light to take pictures and a slower film more light. On the face of it, it might seem best to use a high-speed film but the slower the film, the better the grain and sharpness, the better the print. Most travel photographers equip themselves with films in the region of 50ASA. Generally, films of this speed require good sunlight if the camera is to be hand held otherwise a tripod is required.

Films of 100ASA give adequate results and are often preferred when extra speed helps; for example, when using a telephoto lens. Films of a higher speed are reserved for special situations, close-up work or interior work using natural light.

Making a choice

Top choice for many professionals is Fuji Velvia 50ASA film. It gives good, saturated colours and reproduces excellently. In the

100ASA bracket, Fuji Provia and Fuji Sensia are market leaders.

Kodak too have some leading contenders with Kodak 64ASA and Kodak Elite II at 100ASA. The less vibrant colours of the 64ASA film are preferred by some as perhaps more natural.

All these films offer high specifications and in the end it often boils down to personal preferences and the particular application.

The secret of good photography

There are a few areas which, once understood, will help you on the way to producing a steady stream of quality pictures. These are:

- exposure
- light
- picture composition.

Exposure

More pictures end up in the bin from poor exposure than for any other reason. As already mentioned, modern cameras generally take correctly exposed pictures. There are certain conditions under which they fail to do this and these conditions are especially important to travel photographers.

Certain instructions are built into the camera on manufacture. Regarding exposure, the sum of all the bright parts of a picture combined with all the dark parts equates to grey. More particularly it equates to 18 per cent grey. This works extremely well for the vast majority of scenes. There are circumstances where it does not work, when the scene is largely white, *eg* snow, or largely black.

As far as the travel photographer is concerned, there are many bright scenes where it is necessary to take control of the exposure. Brightly lit beach scenes, white churches, ancient sites in highly reflective marble are all difficult to photograph for the unwary. The solution is quite simple: purchase an 18 per cent grey card from a photographic dealer. Turn the camera to manual, take an exposure reading from the grey card bathed in the same light as the scene and use that reading to take the photograph. The result is a correctly exposed picture.

Grey card exposures can be used in any situation but in most cases it will agree with the camera reading. It leads to a correct exposure when the scene is mainly light or dark.

Light

The quality of the light alone can make a photograph into

something special. Perhaps the most difficult to contend with is the harsh light of bright sunlight around the middle of the day. Early morning and late afternoon are often best when conditions are bright. Some days have a special clarity, usually when bright weather returns after heavy rain, and these days are ideal. It seems that everywhere you point the camera produces a good picture.

With a little awareness, lighting conditions which produce good photographs are quickly recognised. This does not mean that the camera retires every time a cloud appears but it does mean adjusting the type of picture you take to the lighting conditions. When the light is bright and shadows harsh, for example, it may mean using some flash to fill in the shadows.

Picture composition
Many people have a natural ability and can compose an interesting picture without difficulty. It is also a skill which can be learnt or improved simply by studying the work of others. The most useful guide in this respect is the rule of thirds. It often helps to place the principal object in the picture at a distance of one-third along from the side of the picture and one-third from the top or bottom. It works effectively in most cases but sometimes placing the subject right in the middle works equally well, especially when it adds drama to the picture.

Like all skills, picture composition develops with practice until the rules are pushed aside by your own personal interpretation of a scene. When you have reached that point you have become a photographer.

Recognising good pictures
It is easy to think that travel pictures are pictures of either buildings or landscapes. This is far from the truth. Different publishers have different ideas about the type of picture they want to include with the article or book. It pays to study previous work from the same editor to get some idea, but there are a number of pointers which lead in the right general direction. Some tips for taking good travel pictures are offered in Figure 3.

STORING PICTURES

It takes only one or two commissions for slides to mount up. Your films returned from the processing house might arrive neatly packed in small boxes but this is not a good method for general storage.

Tips for good pictures

- Try to make sure that your pictures include **people**. Deserted beaches and ancient ruins uncluttered by hordes are now out of fashion. Pictures should not necessarily be crowded with people but just enough to give atmosphere. Try to ensure that the people are appropriately dressed. For a beach scene, for example, lightly dressed or in bathing costume would be appropriate but walkers in the countryside would be expected to have walking boots and rucksacks.

- **Colour**, deep saturated colour filling much of the frame produces pictures with impact. There is usually plenty of colour around at holiday locations; sun shades, fishing boats, blue sea. Add a few people and there is instantly scope for some good pictures.

- Do not be content with taking just an **overall view**. Look at the detail within the picture to find more interest. For example, a colourful fishing boat on the beach with a fisherman mending his nets would be irresistible. There might be still more pictures, a close-up of the fisherman at work or a close shot of the bow of the boat showing both line and colour.

- Keep shots **tightly cropped** to keep unnecessary distractions out of the scene.

Fig. 3. Tips for good pictures.

When you need to track down a particular slide, it takes an age to open a box and examine every slide one at a time. There are better ways.

Ring binder slide sheets

Transparent sheets holding about 20 slides are freely available from photographic dealers. Slides simply slip into the pockets and the sheet can be stored safely in a ring binder. When choosing a particular slide, just hold a sheet up to the light and 20 slides can be inspected in a moment.

Hangfile slide sheets

This is exactly the same principal as the ring binder sheets except that the sheets are supplied with a hanging bar so that the sheet can be stored suspended in a filing cabinet. This is the ultimate method of storage and particularly useful when large numbers of slides are involved. A single drawer of a standard filing cabinet houses about 5,000 slides.

Filing

It is important to establish a filing system from the outset so that a slide library can be built in an organised manner. Prime requirements of any system are:

* new slides can be added easily
* particular slides are easily found
* returned slides can be replaced in original location.

Filing by year and then by project will cope with most situations but each slide will require a unique map reference in order to refile it.

SUBMITTING PICTURES

The transparent ring-binder sheets used for storing slides are also ideal for sending slides off to a picture editor. Placing the sheet on a light box, it takes the editor only a moment or two to carry out a detailed appraisal and select slides of interest.

Each slide must carry a reference number, name and address and a caption. It might seem a tall order given the small area available on a slide mount but the name and address can always go on the reverse. Coloured circular spots and narrow labels are freely available from leading newsagents, office suppliers and photographic dealers. The spots are handy for the reference number and the labels for a caption. If necessary, a list of slides can be provided with more detailed captions.

Making a list of submitted slides is a good idea from the point of view of keeping a track of where they are rather than relying on memory.

CHECKLIST

* Consider whether your basic photographic equipment is adequate for taking slide films.

* Devise a strategy for improving your photographic skills.

- Consider whether to subscribe to a regular monthly photographic magazine to increase awareness of techniques and equipment.

- Take every opportunity to practise your photography and aim to put together a portfolio of around 24 slides to illustrate the quality of your work.

CASE STUDIES

Caroline worries about photography

Caroline realises that she may be called upon to provide photographs when she starts submitting articles and it is causing her some concern. At the moment she uses a compact camera for taking photographs for the family album and feels she might have a good eye for a picture. She likes taking pictures or rather, if she is honest with herself, she likes seeing the results.

She has been dropping hints steadily to Tom that she would like a better camera for Christmas but she is unsure of which model to buy. Her friend has suggested buying a monthly photographic magazine to be aware of the market and prices. Caroline has decided to go one step further and sign on for a night-school class. All she needs to do now is charm Tom into baby-sitting every Tuesday evening.

Mike and Susan change tack

Mike has always been a keen photographer and has a specialised interest in wild flowers. Whenever they travel, Mike has been more intent on taking pictures of the flowers than of the landscape. His camera is equipped with a special macro lens for close-up work and a number of his flower photographs have already been published in specialist magazines.

Mike realises that landscape work and general travel photography will require some new lenses and some readjustment of technique. Already he and Susan have sat together and projected some of the landscape slides in their collection for a critical assessment. Exposure is one area where they need to be concerned since it is losing them some otherwise useful pictures. Overall, they have no great variety in their pictures and this is something they quickly need to redress. In general they are not worried about producing good photographs but know from experience that it takes time and study to improve weak areas.

Rob takes the second-hand route

Before setting off on his travels to Asia, Rob bought quite cheaply a second-hand Pentax with a standard 50mm lens. He ran a film through the camera before going away to check the camera and give himself a little practice.

Rob put the camera to good use and rapidly became adept at handling it. It was not an autofocus model but he found this no hardship. In the end he found the lack of autofocus worked very much in his favour since second-hand lenses have tumbled in price with the rapid gain in popularity of autofocus cameras. He added a 35–70mm zoom lens and a 28mm wide angle lens to his collection at very little cost while he was on his travels.

Although Rob started with print film, he found this good for pictures of people but not for the magnificent scenery around him. Colour slide film proved much more satisfactory. This switch proved quite fortunate, for the adventure holiday company used one or two of his pictures in their brochure.

Slide storage is already becoming something of a problem. At the moment they are all still in small boxes but this is something which needs sorting out very soon. He plans to start looking at storage options and how he might catalogue his slide library on computer.

3
Making Choices

The aura of glamour surrounding travel attracts masses of people into the industry. Travel writing is no exception. There are vast numbers of would-be journalists constantly attempting to enter the profession. Fortunately, the potential market for travel writers is vast and the industry constantly needs fresh talent and new approaches. To maximise your chance of succeeding in this field it is essential to plan a detailed campaign and use a very structured approach.

Although the market for placing work is quite broad, it does divide quite neatly into three segments:

- travel articles
- travel guides
- travel books.

These are by no means mutually exclusive; indeed a successful travel writer will be working in at least two of these sectors if not all three. When you are starting out, it is vital to concentrate your efforts in just one field. Opportunities to work in other sectors will follow with success in one. So there are choices to be made at the outset.

CONSIDERING THE OPTIONS

Travel articles
This is by far the largest market. There is a huge range of magazines available through general and special interest to women's interest. Virtually all of them are illustrated and most devote some space to travel. Although this sector offers the greatest opportunity for finding an opening, it is highly fragmented. In consequence, it is difficult and time-consuming to research. Research is discussed in the following chapter.

Travel guides
This too is a much larger market than might first appear:

1. There is a steady stream of new books appearing each year which require new authors.

2. Authors are required to contribute to particular chapters.

3. If the original author is not available to write a new edition, the work is farmed out to a new author.

Travel books

Books which appear on the bookshelves as travel literature or just travel books are something apart. These generally relate a personal account of an author's epic journey. They are mostly written in a graphic style recreating vivid images for the reader to enjoy or in a humorous style. The most successful humour is that which sees a funny side to very ordinary situations.

The market for this anecdotal type of book is by no means insignificant. It is dominated by big names and personalities and is the hardest market for a new writer to progress in. Many travel writers aspire to write such books out of personal satisfaction and because they often stay on the bookshelves for many years. Writers of the class of Eric Newby and Freya Stark have seen their books reprinted and reprinted many times over. Unless you are a born storyteller and prepared to make an epic journey, consider the other sectors ahead of this one in the beginning.

THINKING ABOUT FINANCE

Economics may well play a role in shaping your choices. Naturally, for all your work and effort you expect to be paid but you only get paid for success. In writing travel articles you may invest a lot of time and effort in writing articles for submission to various magazines without much to show for your efforts. This you can put down to experience.

When you have managed to place an article you will be paid on the word length of the article at the standard rate offered by the particular publisher. The money may not be paid over until after publication which could take several months. Even if you are successful in placing your first article, it will still take time to establish a flow of income. This is no problem if you have another source of funds.

Authors contemplating writing a travel guide are not advised to proceed without first securing a contract. This will be discussed in more detail later. Publishers normally adopt one of these two payment systems:

- Offer a fixed fee for text and possibly another fee for photographs.
- Pay an initial advance then royalties on book sales.

In either case, the fee or advance will be made as stage payments, some on signing the contract, more on submitting the manuscript and the rest on publication. In the first instance, the exact amount of money you will obtain for the book will be clearly known. On the other hand, the amount received by royalty payments depends on the number of books sold and the shelf life of the book. Imponderable factors which make comparisons difficult. The real difference is that the fee system pays up money relatively quickly whereas the royalty payments continue at a lower level over many years.

FINDING TIME

When it comes to making choices about where and how to start work in this field, time is given little consideration. Writing is an all-consuming business. Sit down in front of a keyboard to do some serious writing and the clock moves at double time. Minutes tick away and speed into hours. In reality, when the writing stage is eventually reached, it may be the quickest part of the job. Research precedes the writing stage. Research is necessary to:

- identify the market
- provide the content.

Each of these stages can take infinitely more time than the writing.

Looking at the short term

With articles and short pieces, work can be slotted in whenever time is available. If you have other employment then the travel writing can be pursued in your spare time. Even with all these restrictions, an article can be produced in a relatively short period of time, days or weeks, compared to a travel guide.

Looking ahead

A whole different time-scale comes into play with travel guides. It is no longer a question of days and weeks but weeks and months.

There are no standards for guidebooks, they can be any length. As a rough indication, a small guide with 40,000 words and freely illustrated with pictures will possibly produce an octavo size book running to 130–140 pages. A medium sized book will run to 80–100,000 words and may have something like 300 pages. Progress can be slow when having to stop to refer back to your notes or reference sources. Checking facts is so important – the height of a mountain, the date the invasion took place, the name of the church or whatever – and it all takes time.

Even working full time on a project, researching the content will take weeks and producing the manuscript, the maps and the supporting illustrations will also take weeks. Your commitment to the project does not end when you hand over the manuscript. Some input will be required during the editorial stages for proof reading if nothing else.

REVIEWING WRITING STYLES

Life would be simpler if the whole spectrum of travel writing demanded the same style. It does not, but the differences cannot easily be slipped into categories. Style is something that varies from magazine to magazine, paper to paper and publisher to publisher. You need to be aware of the differences when starting your market research. This will be discussed later.

There is usually a difference in styles between travel guides and articles. They demand different disciplines. Travel guides serve to inform the reader, provide information and create atmosphere. Look at this example describing Monolithos castle from our *Visitor's Guide to Rhodes*:

> Monolithos castle sits astride Monopetra, a blunted needle of grey rock rising precipitously to 774ft. This is no fairy-tale castle but a real life impregnable fortress built by the Grand Master d'Aubusson. Thick walls thread around the top and inside is the white church of Ag. Panteleimon.

It is packed with information; the name of the castle, the name and height of the rock, the builder and the name of the church are all contained within these few lines. None of this is allowed to distract from creating a vivid picture of the castle.

Travel articles are less constrained by the need to include so much information. There is much more scope for creative writing and above all there is freedom. Freedom to express and develop ideas, freedom to use personal anecdotes to enhance the tale and freedom to let the article take on a life of its own.

Style is nothing more than the way each of us expresses thoughts and ideas using the written word. It is an extension of our personalities. It can be modified and adapted to some extent but, until you have considerable experience, your best work will reflect your own personal style. In the first instance, stay with your natural style and choose the area most likely to suit. This is the way to success.

ANALYSING THE MARKET SEGMENTS

The market for articles and guides is complex and deserving of a more detailed examination. If it is possible to narrow down areas of interest at an early stage, then a great deal of effort and time can be saved in the long run.

Travel writers are there to serve the travel industry and to do so in an impartial manner. However and wherever people spend their holidays, they need information and the job of the travel writer is to meet that need. Holidaymakers need information to open up new ideas for holidays, advice about what to do, what to pack, when to go, how to take care of their money and just about every conceivable aspect of holidaymaking. Any of these aspects can be turned into a travel article. These considerations are really the bottom of the tree so it may be best to start at the top and work down the various branches.

The travel tree
The first division on descending the tree asks if you wish to work in the home market or the overseas market. Whichever branch you follow, the next division poses the same question – local, regional or countrywide? This already represents six different areas of the market and each branch still has further divisions. The final division determines how these areas may be treated – in a general way, using a theme or pursuing a special interest. These various pathways are shown in Figure 4.

If you choose to work in the home market then local and regional spring to mind as the obvious starting point for guides or articles. Looking overseas, it might seem appropriate to think in terms of a new country guide but your research will soon show there are already guides for virtually every country in the world and most islands. Some countries are covered by as many as thirty books all by different publishers. This sector of the market is nearing

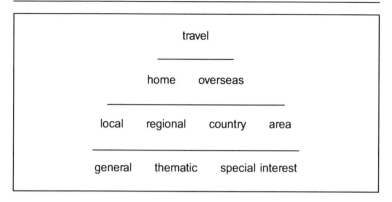

Fig. 4. The travel tree.

saturation point but there may still be opportunities in writing new editions. There is still some mileage in regional guides which cover just part of a country but in more detail, such as northern Italy or southern Spain.

The bottom line of the tree indicates different ways the task of writing the article or guide might be interpreted. General here means a straightforward approach describing places and events in whatever style is appropriate. The terms thematic and special interest need a little more expansion.

Thematic

This area of travel writing is one which challenges the imagination and offers huge scope for originality. Almost any theme which acts as a thread on which to string the whole can be used. Historical themes are constantly popular, such as following in the footsteps of Alexander the Great, rediscovering the Silk Road or Moorish Spain. The variety is endless and it does not necessarily have to be a grand theme, you could just as easily write about the clog makers of Lancashire. Car tours are universally popular. *The Scenic Highways of Europe*, for example, uses this as a theme. Similarly, accommodation offers scope as in farm holidays or perhaps the Paradors of Spain. Food and wine make popular themes, as people are always in search of different eating places. The opportunities here are limitless.

Special interest

Special interest holidays have been a major growth area over the past few years and there is plenty of scope here for new writers. Walking holidays both at home and abroad have been around for many years and there is plenty of literature available. Other interests are less supported. People go cruising, ski, windsurf, play bridge, play golf, fish, cycle, mountain bike, scuba dive, watch birds, look for wild flowers, search for antiques, take unusual train journeys and so on.

Not every journalist is willing to go mountain biking or has the knowledge to join an antiques chase and this is where someone with special interest can gain an advantage and enter into the field of travel writing.

Overviewing the market

This overview of the market may be simplistic. Its boundaries merge into other disciplines all too often. Tips to avoid sunburn might equally come under health, or best deals on holiday insurance might be more appropriate on business pages, but they do appear under travel. All this simply underscores the complexity of the market place. There are clear messages to take aboard now before starting on serious market research otherwise a lot of time may be wasted. You need to:

- Focus on the breadth of the market. This increases your scope for producing new ideas.

- Pick out themes or approaches from pieces of work which have particular appeal to you.

- Use lateral thinking to translate those ideas to the areas in which you plan to write.

CHECKLIST

- Decide which area of travel writing appeals to you most.

- Make a plan of how you are going to finance yourself for the project you have in mind.

- Decide which sector of the market offers the best opportunity for your skills.

- Devise a positive plan of action for the project you have in mind.

CASE STUDIES

Caroline realises her limitations

Circumstances have dictated most of Caroline's decisions. She knows that she is limited to working in her own locality in the main. Fortunately, she has a car and can get out and about to do her research and Tom is supportive and happy to use weekends to visit photographic locations. The family normally takes its holidays abroad. Caroline appreciates that with forethought and planning these could easily provide more material for producing articles.

With two young children, time is something of a problem. Now that the younger one has started at nursery school three mornings a week and with the elder attending school, she knows that she will have some quiet hours for writing. Much of it will probably be done in the evening when the children are in bed. Although she would like to write a guide and plans to in the future, she knows at the moment she cannot give such a project the time it needs. She has decided to set such ideas aside for now and concentrate on articles.

Mike and Susan work things out

Faced with too many choices, Mike and Susan realise they need to narrow down their options. Denied the opportunity to travel in their youth, they are keen to spend time overseas. It is in this area that they have decided to concentrate their thoughts. With all their children now married, they have all the time they need to throw themselves into a new career which is exactly what they plan to do. In the short term, money is no problem, Mike has a pension which is adequate for the moment but he knows it will lose its buying power over the years. He must think of supplementing it in the foreseeable future. The idea of writing books and being paid on a royalty basis to build up a second pension has considerable appeal.

They would like to work on mainstream travel guides but realise their lack of experience will make this difficult. Mike and Susan have had many discussions about the problem of landing their first contract and have decided on a strategy. They plan to use their knowledge and expertise to try first at the special interest end of the market. With a scientific background, Mike knows the value of an ordered approach and suggests that they start by listing their combined skills and interests. The list looks like this:

- photography
- walking

- countryside
- history
- wild flowers.

When they start to research the market, they will be concentrating their efforts on the type of guide which will make best use of their particular interests.

Rob recognises his problems

Money is a big problem for Rob. He knows that whatever he does, it must be on a fee-earning basis. There is the possibility of a small bank loan but it is something he wants to avoid. He has spoken to the lecturer at the college where he is studying and knows that some publishers prefer to pay fees rather than a royalty. The lecturer explained that these are usually the bigger companies which employ a large number of authors. Rob is aware that this will be a key aspect of his research which he must resolve before he can shape further plans.

Continuity is something of a problem; he would like to have a project in place to follow on from the completion of his studies in six months' time. He knows that he needs to start looking for work straight away to achieve this. In the meantime, he intends to write travel articles for projects on his writing course so that he can take advantage of the lecturer's advice and guidance.

4
Researching the Market

If there is one rock upon which the efforts of new writers founder, it is the failure to research the market-place adequately. This is true not just for travel writing but for virtually every field where writers wish to be published. No matter how good the writing, no matter how skilful the construction, no matter how long it took to compose the piece, it will not be published unless it serves the needs of the market.

There is no point in writing a travel article or book of your dreams and then trying to find a publisher – the industry does not work in that manner. Research is the way to open doors but there is a whole new learning curve ahead. As frustrating as it might seem, taking time to gain an insight into the world of publishing, its current trends and its requirements will pay rich dividends.

Understanding the advantages of good research

To stress the value of thoroughly conducted research, look at some of the general advantages that can accrue:

- It ensures you waste nobody's time, neither yours nor editors, with unnecessary and ill-directed work.

- It brings you up to date with current styles and trends.

- It reveals the full scope of the market for travel-related topics.

- It allows you to appreciate the individual approaches of the various magazines and newspapers.

- It helps you to develop lateral thinking and formulate new ideas and approaches.

The prime purpose of all this research is to ensure that your work is specifically designed to meet a market already identified and that the work is delivered at an appropriate time. Timing is a subject which will be touched on later but, by way of example, there is little point in submitting a topical article on skiing when the season is all but over.

DEFINING YOUR OBJECTIVES

Before starting the research phase, it is important to think about what you want to learn from it. This allows you to build comprehensive records right from the start. Unfortunately, there is often a chicken and egg situation at the beginning since you do not know exactly what there is to find. The way to overcome this difficulty is to make a preliminary start on the research and use the information gathered to refine your approach before starting in earnest.

Narrowing the field

Although you need to be aware of all the market opportunities in travel writing, it is impractical to thoroughly research the whole field. Chapter 3 looked at market segments and some of the choices that can be made. Now is the time to crystallise thinking into definite preferences and to focus on the information needed.

Collecting information

Although each project will have its own particular requirements, some broad guidelines can be offered for the sort of information that might be needed. The markets for travel guides and articles are quite different and need to be considered separately.

Travel guides

Finding out which publishers are involved in producing travel guides is an obvious first step. Source material will be discussed shortly but a classified list of publishers found under the heading of travel is not usually a short cut. Publishers with only a tenuous connection with travel seem invariably to dominate these listings. Start by making your own list and find out the area of interest of each publisher. Only major publishers tend to cover world-wide destinations, most others specialise in particular areas. Some may be totally dedicated to niche markets or special interests but it is important to record all this information.

A sample record card is shown in Figure 5 which indicates the sort of information which needs to be collected in the first instance. Building a profile of a particular publisher is discussed in a later chapter.

```
┌─────────────────────────────────────────────────────────────┐
│                   Travel Guide Publishers                      │
│                                                                │
│  Company:.....................   Travel editor:.....................│
│  Areas of interest:...............  Catalogue: ......................│
│  ..................................  ..................................│
│  ..................................  ..................................│
│  Series titles: ....................  Type of illustrations:...........│
│  ..................................  ..................................│
│                                                                │
└─────────────────────────────────────────────────────────────┘
```

Fig. 5. Sample travel guide record card.

With all the take-overs and consolidation in recent years, many well-known publishing names are part of a bigger concern. Usually they continue to trade under their former names and continue with an independent editor and staff so it has little consequence in practical terms.

Travel articles
Consumer magazines are now enormous in their scope and number. Very few are actually devoted entirely to travel but most have a travel section of some kind. Unfortunately, many magazines use staff and not freelance writers for their travel sections. Finding out is not always easy but some reference books (see below) do give this sort of information. Inspecting the magazine can give clues. Look for by-lines – staff writers do not usually get credit but check anyway in the staff list at the front.

It is especially important to identify the readership. Magazines attempt to identify and target a particular group of people. It may be the young twenties, the chic thirties or perhaps a more mature readership. Obviously, travel articles published will be appropriate for their readers. An upmarket women's magazine might run an article on shopping in New York while windsurfing on Mallorca would be more suited to a magazine aimed at the young and active.

Monthly magazines obviously offer more scope for articles than quarterlies. Editorial content, especially on travel, is usually planned about two or three copies in advance. It means waiting about a year to get work into a quarterly publication.

Consumer Magazines

Magazine:.................   Frequency: ....   Editor:.........

Readership:...............   Freelance contributors: yes/no

....

Travel content:............   Type of article: ....

....

Fig. 6. Sample consumer magazine record card.

The record card shown in Figure 6 is a good starting point for collecting information, but it will probably need to be modified to satisfy your particular enquiries.

The world of magazines is fairly mobile. New titles appear, some not-so-old titles disappear and others redesign themselves or change their market appeal. Having done your market research, the magazines of interest to you will have reduced considerably and keeping an eye on changes is then not such a daunting task.

Knowing an editor's name is essential but with so many changes it is difficult to keep track. The most certain way is to make a telephone enquiry before submitting any work.

Noting advertisers

Few magazines can survive without running adverts. They bring income and help to keep the cost down to the consumer. The adverts generate income for the advertiser. In other words they need each other so it is beneficial to both parties to work hand in hand. If a holiday company wants to promote its Greek holidays, then it would ask the magazine when it plans to run an article on Greece and advertise in that issue.

This works in two ways:

1. A magazine gathers in its advertisers then turns to freelances to provide the supporting material. This can be hard on freelance writers. Deadlines are often short and there is limited time to research and write the article.

2.   In the opposite approach, a magazine lays out its editorial
     content for the next six months, commissions the articles and
     then looks for supporting advertisers.

Only one or two magazines fall exclusively in one category or the
other; most fall somewhere in between. Noting the adverts can give
a clue to what might be needed and when. Articles on popular
Mediterranean destinations make a regular appearance each year in
mid-winter just as tour operators are gearing up to sell holidays.
Winter destinations are promoted in late summer. Once you have
established the pattern of advertising in a newspaper or magazine,
you can start to appreciate the type of articles needed and when.

CHECKING REFERENCE SOURCES

There are some very useful books available in the market-place
which take a lot of the hard work out of market research. Be sure to
work with only the latest editions since they date so quickly. Most
are revised annually and make their appearance on the bookshelves
by October for the following year. Libraries often stock them or will
get them to order.
     You should consider:

• *Writers' and Artists' Yearbook* (annual, A & C Black). This book,
  perhaps the best known on the market, has just passed its 90th
  birthday. It is a treasure trove of information on publishers of all
  types, covering books, magazines and newspapers both in the UK
  and overseas English-speaking countries. There are usually a
  number of articles helpful to new writers which are well worth
  reading. Photographers will find a directory of agencies and
  picture libraries.

• *The Writer's Handbook* (annual, Macmillan). Another equally
  fine treasure trove which has similar listings to the above but with
  slightly different information. Somehow they manage to comple-
  ment each other and checking on a particular publisher in both
  books usually gives a more complete picture. Again the articles
  are helpful to writers and are well worth reading. Photographers
  are catered for with listings of picture libraries.

• *The Freelance Photographer's Market Handbook* (annual, BFP
  Books – Bureau of Freelance Photographers). Although intended

primarily for photographers seeking markets, it has an excellent listing of UK consumer magazines with plenty of information valuable to writers.

- *Photographer's Market* (annual, Writer's Digest Books). This is exclusively devoted to markets in the USA and contains a vast amount of information on consumer magazines and photographic libraries.

Public Libraries tend to be a bit slow in keeping up to date with annual directories. However, editions from earlier years can still be useful for their articles.

Visiting the library

While libraries do not always have the same comprehensive stocks of travel guides or magazines seen in bookshops, they should not be dismissed. Nobody minds if you sit there for hours browsing and making notes – that is what libraries are for. Pick out the more recent travel guides and:

- look to see if other titles are listed
- study the style
- work out the intended market
- look for photographs and read the credits
- fill in a record card.

Do not overlook the indexes which will provide a full list of titles held by the library although some may be out on loan. Be sure to request any titles you wish to read. These will be obtained for you even if that title is not held at the branch.

Similarly, with magazines concentrate on the travel articles and:

- look for by-lines
- check to see if the writers are staff
- look for supporting pictures
- check quality and credits
- fill in a record card.

Visiting bookshops

A good bookshop may have many shelves devoted to travel guides and be quite overwhelming. Narrowed down to your area of interest, the task is less daunting. It is not quite as easy for making notes as the library but try and jot down some information for your records.

Bookshops often offer the best opportunity to look at competitive titles for a given destination. If there are 20 or 30 fairly recent titles for a particular country, there is not a great chance of persuading a publisher that a new title is needed. This rush into titles when a new destination opens up is by no means uncommon. It happens all the time. Publishers then find their sales are not good because of the intense competition so fail to carry on with new editions. Some ten or 15 years further on, the books are all out of date and new opportunities open up for travel writers and publishers.

Magazine displays can also be daunting but the best way to research these is on a little and often basis. Some you may wish to buy to study further but in the first instance a quick scan is all that is required. Keeping notes is vital to avoid wasting time and going over the same ground.

Collecting catalogues

Book publishers large and small invariably produce a catalogue which they will supply on request. These are an invaluable source of information for book writers. They offer complete listings of all series they publish and give some insight into the character of each. Not only does it bring you right up to date but if often publicises books due for publication. This insight into the direction in which a publisher is moving is especially useful when you reach the stage of formulating a proposal. Similarly, studying the titles in a particular series might suggest opportunities for new titles.

Surfing the net

The Internet is rapidly becoming an invaluable research tool for travel related topics. Travel destinations, hotels, books and magazines are already widely promoted on the Internet but this is still only the tip of the iceberg. Improvements in the organisation of information, in the search engines for browsing and in the speed of access are taking place steadily. This will attract still more users to advertise their services so it is set to become even more useful.

Anyone with a suitable computer fitted with a modem and access to a telephone point can gain access to the Internet. Once you have signed on with a service provider, such as American On Line, CompuServe or BT, there is a world of information available to you immediately from your own home or office.

CHECKLIST

- Decide which areas of the market to research.

- Plan the information you need to collect.

- Start a recording or filing system for the information gathered.

- Design a record card to suit your project.

- Be prepared to revise your approach based on what you learn.

- Plan ahead to keep your records ongoing.

- Be sure to include all sources of information.

CASE STUDIES

Caroline has problems

Caroline intends to make a start by writing about her own locality. Living as she does on the borders of Devon and Cornwall, there will be no shortage of interesting material. She would like to market her work both locally and nationally.

Living in a rural area has its attractions but she regrets the lack of good research facilities. Caroline is a regular visitor to the local library and makes good use of their services. Her only grumble is that it can sometimes take weeks to order and receive a particular book or reference paper. The alternative is a trip into town which she does occasionally for major shopping expeditions. Caroline knows that researching takes time, too long to fit into a shopping trip, so it will mean special excursions when necessary.

Caroline is no stranger to the Internet since she and her husband Tom are regular users. She is hoping that the Internet will offer considerable help in finding out about publishers and magazines. This is particularly attractive to her since it is home based and can be done later in the evening when the children are in bed. The other part of her plan is to build up a good reference library at home.

Mike and Susan browse the bookshelves

Mike and Susan have already decided that their efforts in the first instance will be directed to writing guidebooks. It was no great surprise to their friends since both Mike and Susan always seem to have their noses buried in some bookshop or other. They also collect books, both new and second-hand, and already have an effective reference library in their favourite subjects. Browsing the shelves is where they will start their research.

Both know well enough the limitations of this approach since only dedicated travel bookshops can ever carry anything approaching comprehensive stock. Having in the past picked up some instore catalogues for travel guides, they appreciate this is another source of information to explore. Susan always carries a small notebook in her handbag which she uses to make notes when away from home. She is particularly meticulous at keeping notes and records.

The *Writers' and Artists' Yearbook* is already on their bookshelf at home and they intend to check for similar reference books. They feel particularly comfortable with the task of researching the market and are quite prepared to leave no stone unturned.

Rob gets help

Rob is progressing well on his journalism course and getting a great deal of support and help from his tutor. Since his tutor is also a professional journalist he is getting plenty of sound advice about the state of the market and on the problems of marketing himself.

The college library is well stocked with books on writing and journalism, including a range of reference books like *The Writer's Handbook*. Checking up on publishers in the latter book, Rob has noticed comments on royalty payments in some instances. This is particularly valuable information for him since circumstances dictate that he must start his career earning fees rather than royalties. Checking through the publishers involved in travel and eliminating those paying royalties will appreciably cut the list. This will make his work load lighter when he is ready to find out more about individual publishers.

As part of his course work, Rob is keen to try his hand at writing articles based on his Asia travels for publication. Again his tutor is familiar with the market-place and has already suggested some magazines where he might place his work. The library has several issues so he has been busy looking at the style, content and length of the travel articles. If he can get something published, it will boost his confidence and look good on his CV.

5
Formulating an Idea

At some stage in the process and before settling down to write serious articles, you will need to find something to write about. Plucking an idea out of thin air rarely happens unless you know your subject thoroughly. In this case one idea is not going to forge a new career. You will need to produce a steady stream of themes and ideas attractive to publishers. This is never more daunting than when first beginning.

After a thrilling day out in Blackpool, it might seem like a good idea to write an article about it so everybody can enjoy your experience. It is doomed to fail. The skill is to identify the current needs of the market and match your ideas to it. This is the way to success.

Time spent on market research will start to pay rich dividends once you have a clear focus and are working to a definite objective. Inevitably, a considerable amount of trial and error is involved initially. Later on, with a greater involvement in the travel industry, ideas and opportunities flow from your work, from contacts in the industry, from press releases and a whole range of sources.

While inspiration cannot always be produced to order, it is important to channel your energies in the right direction to make sure they are not wasted.

HAVING A FOCUS

The advice in Chapter 3 was to explore the breadth of the travel market to understand the opportunities it offers and perhaps gain inspiration and ideas. This advice still holds but there comes a time when it is necessary to focus on the areas which attract you most. It is a natural step on the way to producing ideas and turning them into practice. When you start to delve more deeply into a chosen area it is often thought provoking in itself. New ideas are formed simply by introducing lateral thinking from your wider research.

The messages here are quite simple:

- Stay abreast of the whole industry.

- Keep your own interests to the front of your mind.

- Use lateral thinking to bring ideas from other areas into your field of interest.

Writing about things you know

This advice is commonly offered to new writers and it holds true throughout the whole spectrum of writing. It is very important to feel confident about your subject and demonstrate control.

If you have specialised knowledge, do not hesitate to use it. This is one way to set yourself apart from, and gain advantage over, journalists already working in the industry. Train buffs might have opportunities to write about great little train journeys, bird watchers about over-wintering birds in the UK, walkers about canal walks and so on. There are always opportunities but the secret of success is recognising them.

Some specialisation might be necessary in the beginning to get started. It is nothing to be concerned about. Wherever the starting point, your work and ideas will evolve and lead eventually into quite different areas which you could not have envisaged at the start. The best calling card is a publication. Once over that hurdle, it becomes a little easier to make progress and to start changing direction.

Keeping your ideas simple

Ideas do not necessarily have to have grand themes or sweep the reader across several continents. That might come later. Keep things simple in the beginning. Look at other articles and analyse them for the scope and content. Look also for the theme of the article and decide on the idea behind it. It is an exercise well worth doing. Articles in the main are limited in scope but usually have an underlying theme. Blackpool can be used again as an example of this point. Instead of writing about a day out, write about Blackpool Tower using the activities which take place within the tower as an underlying theme. It might stand more chance of getting published.

Keeping your ideas commercial

While it is always appealing to write about something which you find interesting or attractive, the editor's chief concern is whether it will sell the publication. To do this it must have wide appeal (unless it is for a specialist publication), be supported by advertising or generally enhance the quality.

Look at it from an editor's point of view. The question they ask themselves is whether this contribution will help to sell their publication. Big names well known to the public will do just that but everybody else has to make their work talk for them.

Topical items are often well received provided you can stay ahead of the pack, otherwise this type of item dies rapidly. Countries like Greece and Spain have had so much written about them that it is easy to imagine there is no room for another article or book. Every spring newspapers are full of articles on all the popular Mediterranean destinations for the simple reason that they attract masses of adverts from tour companies.

TIMING CAN BE CRITICAL

Submitting an article

Hitting a publisher with the right idea at the right time can be critical. A simple example is that of the seasonal flow of articles in the newspapers. Returning to the spring deluge of travel articles on popular destinations, the problem is knowing when to make a submission. This sort of campaign is planned by travel editors weeks in advance so the advertisers can be alerted. If your article falls on the editor's desk when this campaign is being formulated and it fits into the general theme, you are onto a winner.

Unless you already work with or are close to an editor, this information is not forthcoming so you will need to use your own judgement on when to submit. Your research should have alerted you to the pattern of these seasonal articles so plan your own work six to eight weeks in advance.

Magazines are even more difficult to second guess for timing submissions. Clearly their editorial content is sorted out well in advance. In some cases travel topics can be months ahead, even as long as a year. This is the case when a magazine is not driven by adverts but still needs the support of advertisers. It puts out its programme well in advance and hopes the adverts roll in.

The other approach is much more short term. A backbone of travel items may be pencilled in well ahead but when advertisers place adverts, the magazine responds by finding a suitable article. If there happens to be one lying in the editor's slush pile then it will be snatched up with glee. Otherwise the editor rushes around asking regular freelance authors for suitable articles.

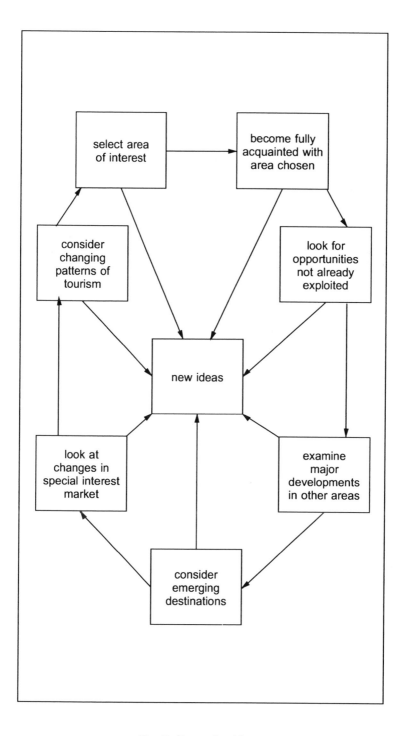

Fig. 7. Generating ideas.

Submitting a travel guide proposal

There is an element of timing too with travel guide publishers. The book trade is growing more and more international and the opportunity to sell a book to other countries either in the English language or in translation never more important. Frankfurt hosts the biggest book fair in the world every October and this provides a forum for publishers to get together and trade.

Trading is done not just in published books but also in ideas. Speculative proposals for new titles submitted to publishers throughout the previous months are often discussed with prospective buyers at this trade fair. If a particular proposal is well received then the publisher returns ready to commission. Sometimes ideas do not meet the exact commercial needs of another country and are modified in discussion.

OPENING FILES

Starting an ideas file

Right from the first moment of starting, it is a good idea to open a file for ideas. Jot down thoughts, ideas, partially formed ideas and suggestions. This file itself, as it builds up, can be a source of fresh inspiration so the more you write the more useful it becomes. Earlier thoughts and partial ideas often take on a new lease when matched with current thinking.

This does not need to be a paper file, it can just as easily be done on computer.

Keeping information files

No industry produces as much paper as the travel industry. Leaflets, brochures and press releases appear almost daily. Some of these will be useful and may need to be retained which means starting some kind of filing system which allows quick access.

This file will almost certainly need to be a paper collection. The sheer volume of material makes it an overwhelming task to transfer to a computer even with the aid of a scanner device. Inexpensive cardboard box files are ideal with a separate file for each location or source of material. Be selective and do not hesitate to cut and paste to ensure that the files are kept only for relevant material. Make a point of reviewing these files fairly frequently since travel material can date fairly quickly.

KEEPING ABREAST OF THE INDUSTRY

Awareness of the industry as a whole is not just a vital part of the learning process but important for formulating ideas. Knowing where to look for information is covered in this section but knowing what to look for follows in the next section.

Work done already in researching the market looking for publishers and outlets for your work will have given you a good flavour of the industry. It may have already produced plenty of ideas but there are other sources which are just as important.

Visiting travel shows

Travel shows are held at major centres throughout the spring months. They are a show case for National Tourist Offices and travel companies and a good place to gain information and leaflets. Much of the value will be lost if you simply drift around, look at exhibits and pick up leaflets. It is a great opportunity to talk travel with the experts. Stop whenever there is a chance to talk:

- present your card
- ask about latest developments in their sector
- express interest in press releases
- ask to go on their mailing list.

Let the conversation flow from there and do not hesitate to make a few notes since you are likely to have many different conversations crowded into your visit. Remember the vested interest of the people you talk to. It is easy to be carried away by their enthusiasm and sales pitch.

The World Travel Market

The largest event in the show calendar is the World Travel Market held in Earl's Court in London every November. More than 160 countries exhibit, just about every National Tourist Office is represented, more than 20,000 exhibitors are on hand and the catalogue alone runs to over 400 pages. A number of travel publishers are also present.

Britain is well represented and all the regional tourist boards are present in force. It is an unrivalled opportunity to find out about developments and opportunities in the home market with every-thing under one roof.

The show is strictly for the trade and usually runs for four days with the first two days by special invitation. The press is included in this invitation. There is usually no admittance for the general public but those genuinely involved in travel are welcome. Publishers are invited to apply for tickets so if you are working for a publisher, no matter how loosely, express an interest and they will get you a ticket. There is no cost involved. Travel agents can also apply for tickets so try your local agent and explain your interest. Otherwise write to the organisers.

Allow at least two days for the show. Getting around can be slow and there are so many events and stands that you will need to be well organised and selective.

Contacting National Tourist Offices
These are always good sources of information and always willing to provide leaflets and brochures. Be specific with your requests otherwise you will simply get a general spread of leaflets. If you have secured a commission for a book or article, do not hesitate to contact their Press Officer for any particular material or help. If you are interested in receiving press releases, let them know.

Learning from newspapers
It is always a good idea to keep an eye on the travel sections of the broadsheets. Apart from articles which are sometimes useful to collect, there are often snippets of information about changes in the travel industry. It is usually possible to pick up on changes in the industry and keep up with current trends.

FINDING THE LEADING EDGE

Whilst visiting travel shows and generally finding out about the travel industry, be sure to keep an eye open for current market trends. The industry may appear fairly static to the outsider but that is far from reality. Change is almost continuous. Some of it is obvious and is well signalled in the press, but you may have to dig a little deeper to unearth the quieter but equally important drifts. If you can pick up the trends quickly, you can keep your articles or your work topical and interesting. It sometimes introduces that little extra which catches a publisher's eye.

Discovering growth areas
There are always new growth areas to unearth. Some of the major ones in recent years include:

1. The explosive growth in holidays to Florida.

2. The increase in long haul holidays to far away, exotic locations.

3. Increasing popularity of leisure cruising to all destinations but particularly to the Caribbean.

All those were well signalled eventually in the press. Some change is a lot slower and is less easily detected. One example is the slow but steady increase in special interest holidays over the past few years. Walking holidays provided by specialist holiday companies have always been popular. More recently, a number of major tour operators, like Thomson, have started to include walking holidays as part of their spring programme for a number of destinations. Similarly, there has been an increase in the number of holidays on offer for painters, lovers of wild flowers, gardeners, bird watchers and even archaeologists.

Holiday formulae
The way in which people spend their holidays is slowly changing too. One of the big changes which has taken place recently is in the growth of all-inclusive holidays, where everything is paid for in the initial price. Such holidays include full board and wine or beer with meals, free excursions and entertainment and sometimes a free bar.

Self-guided walking holidays have now made an appearance. This is for people who want to visit a new location, enjoy a walk without a leader or the company of others. The holiday company sets up a programme of walks, produces a leaflet for each walk for its clients and then makes all the flight, hotel and transfer arrangements. Armed with this information, the clients are simply sent on their way.

The package holiday served to introduce overseas holidays to the mass market. Now, the trend is for people to use the convenience and low cost of these but break away on arrival to follow their own interests and pursuits.

Looking at holiday brochures
This is not the easiest way to do research because of the huge volume of brochures available on the market. Nevertheless, it is often worth a flick through the contents pages looking for new destinations. Often these are highlighted in some way so they are not difficult to pick out. Individually, the new destinations may not be

of much interest but should they turn up in other brochures there may be something interesting to write about.

Goa turned up as a destination this way a year or two back and a travel journalist spotted the absence of a travel guide. Within a year there was a guide on the bookshelves which proved a good selling title for a time until the competition caught up.

Chatting with the customer

Looking at the industry from the other side can sometimes be very helpful. Talk to people and find out what they think on travel topics. Ask if travel guides, articles or holiday programmes on TV fail them. Ask why, ask what changes they would like to see. Get some interesting debates going and if it all works well you will get plenty of new thoughts and ideas. If it is interesting enough, write an article about it.

Discussions like that can be held around the fireside at home but do exactly the same when you are out on location. Encourage people to talk and listen carefully to their views. Prompt them with suggestions of your own but let them do most of the talking.

Going out on location

No matter how much research was conducted beforehand, no matter how much thought went into the trip, the event itself invariably opens up new ideas. This is not necessarily because the trip itself is stimulating but because of unforeseen events, like finding yourself in the middle of a sausage festival, or in unexpected places.

If you already have a commission for an article it means that the editor was happy with the original suggestion. Either you can amend your approach to writing the article or use the new material and ideas for other articles. Ideally, you need to be placing two or three articles from a trip to make it pay so the more ideas and leads the better.

CHECKLIST

- Make plans to organise and file the flood of information and travel leaflets.

- Devise a system for logging and updating your ideas.

- Find out about travel shows in your area.

- Contact National or Regional Tourist Offices for information for your project.

- Make a plan to keep informed on the changes taking place in the tourist industry.

- Try out some consumer research on your friends.

CASE STUDIES

Caroline gets organised

With her experience in management, Caroline appreciates the importance of having information to hand and knowing exactly where to find things. Filing is second nature. She has already made space and opened files to collect leaflets and other useful information. She has set aside a special telephone and address book to collect the names of useful contacts. The local Tourist Office is down in the book and she expects many more to follow.

The value of writing about what you know has not escaped her. She does know that travelling with children and finding suitable accommodation can be a little problematic. This theme she might well write about so whenever she is making enquiries she tries to raise this aspect. Caroline plans to visit the Regional Tourist Office to find out if they have a separate list of facilities which provide for children in her part of the country.

Travel shows have too much of an international flavour for Caroline's interests and she does not think the effort of getting there would be worthwhile. At the moment she is busy reading magazines, newspaper articles and local guidebooks as her source of inspiration and is beginning to note down some ideas for future reference.

Mike and Susan shape up their ideas

With their research so far, Mike and Susan have decided that walking books may well be the way for them to get started. It will bring into use their interests in wild flowers, photography and the countryside.

Before they can think of approaching a publisher, they still have a few problems to solve. The first of these is to find an overseas location which offers the potential of good, safe walking which is convenient and easy to reach. A further requirement is that there must already be a healthy level of tourism to that destination to support the book sales. They know that a publisher will consider the economics of any proposal above all other considerations.

They have discovered little in the way of competitive books and feel there is a good opening if they can identify an attractive destination. Armed with this knowledge, they intend to spend time at the World Travel Market. The plan is to talk to the various National Tourist Offices and find out about the regions which offer good walking potential and to collect information.

Rob makes plans

Living and studying in London, Rob is well placed to attend the World Travel Market. His lecturer has already applied for an allocation of student tickets so Rob is intent on spending some time there.

He has had some experience in Indonesia when he worked for a holiday company and has also visited Vietnam. It is these areas he intends to concentrate on and collect as much information as possible. One idea at the back of his mind is to write something about the Silk Route – this he would find really exciting. Discussions with his tutor on this idea brought a sharp reminder on the economic realities of life. He might choose a title which he would dearly like to do but a publisher will only support the project if it has good prospects of making money.

Rob has taken aboard the message that ideas should be both desirable and commercial but has still not dismissed the Silk Route idea. This is firmly pencilled into his ideas file but he is intent on adding others. He is looking forward to the chance to talk to some of the major book publishers at the show but his tutor thinks their stands will not be fronted by the right people. His advice is to wait for the London Book Fair to talk to publishers.

6
Selling Travel Articles

There comes a time to put pen to paper. In the logical sequence of events, this time arrives only after exploring the complexity of the market-place and identifying possible opportunities for placing articles. Keeping an eye on the market and finding new outlets is an ongoing exercise so it becomes a matter of judgement at which point to try your hand. The right time is when you feel that your work is sensibly targeted at the right readership in the correct market sector.

Before settling down to write, it is necessary to decide on a strategy. There are basically two approaches:

1. Write articles and submit them speculatively in the hope that they will catch the eye of the travel editor. These are known as 'on specs' in the trade.

2. Try first to obtain a commission before writing the article.

These two strategies are not mutually exclusive and it is sensible to pursue both approaches.

SUBMITTING ON SPECS

This speculative approach sometimes works but there is no guarantee of success. It is nice to believe that the quality of the work will catch the editor's eye and ensure publication. Your work should always be of your highest standard both in quality and presentation and, in the end, it may pay dividends.

Going into the slush pile
Travel editors receive speculative submissions daily and they end up in a stack which is referred to as the slush pile. All of them receive attention in time. It does take time and it may be weeks or months before a reply is received.

Taking a chance

Chance plays a part in the articles selected. If the editor is planning a large spread on the Manchester area in advance of an international sporting event, for example, and a speculative article arrives about eating places of character in and around Manchester, it will be received with open arms. Second guessing the editor is about as reliable as backing horses but it does work sometimes. By imagining yourself in the editor's chair and looking at an events calendar, it is possible to anticipate possible areas of interest.

Hoping quality is noticed

Quality work does not go unnoticed even if it is not taken up immediately. The editor will at least make a mental note of the author and, if further work appears on the editor's desk of the same quality, it may bring rewards in either publication or a commission.

Writing speculative articles does provide practice which is both necessary and advisable. Do not be in a rush to submit them. Put them aside for a time until you have forgotten the content then read them with fresh eyes. It is surprising how much you can improve your work by this simple technique.

Making the submission

Submit your work only to one editor at a time. Do not be tempted to take a short cut and send the same article around to five or six editors. If the article is good enough to catch the attention of one editor, it may also attract another. The same piece appearing in different newspapers or magazines at more or less the same time is a short cut to terminating a promising career.

There is no harm in circulating different articles, indeed it is the most sensible approach. Be sure to keep a record of your submissions similar to that shown in Figure 8.

Fig. 8. Sample projects record.

Extend the record by adding each article sent out and keep a copy by the telephone. Responses sometimes come by telephone so it is vital to be sure exactly who is on the phone, especially when you have a number of submissions floating around.

Submitting articles on spec is a hard testing ground for writers entering the profession but a necessary one. Hours of work can reap little in the way of financial reward but the occasional successes are especially valuable for building a portfolio. Once you can approach a publisher with some recent publications to your name, there is far more chance of obtaining commissions.

OBTAINING COMMISSIONS

Approaching an editor

The wrong way
It might seem like a good idea to ring up the travel editor with the news that you are off to New Zealand shortly and ask about the possibilities of writing a piece. Editors are extremely busy people and, unless your work is known to the editor, it is highly unlikely that a commission will be agreed over the phone. A curt refusal is the most likely outcome but a more polite editor might ask exactly what you intend to write about and then ask you to put it in writing.

The right way
Since a telephone call risks irritating the editor into dismissing you promptly, the best approach is to write in with your ideas in the first place. Setting them down on paper makes sure that the ideas are sensibly thought out and properly presented. The accompanying letter provides the opportunity to introduce yourself and your work and may be retained on file for future reference.

PRESENTING IDEAS

While you are taking the trouble to write to an editor, you might as well present a number of themes for articles to offer a wider choice. There is no magic number but six ideas gives a better chance than one and remains within an editor's concentration span. Too many ideas or ideas with too much detail risk not being fully examined.

Being brief
Remember, you are not writing the article at this stage, just a short

synopsis. The editor wants to assess the basic story-line and decide whether the approach is suitable and interesting for the magazine or paper's readership. The length is always a matter of judgement depending on the amount of information you need to convey. If it runs to a full page then it is more than likely too long.

Example
Using New Zealand again as an example, the following is the type of idea which might succeed aimed at the right market:

> New Zealand on a budget, staying in Youth Hostels.
> There are some 59 youth hostels spread over both North and South islands offering a high level of comfort and suitable for all ages. The city hostels even offer airport connections for arriving and departing visitors and country locations offer exciting opportunities for adventure from glacier rafting to horse trekking. Travel Pass packages are available which include airport pickup, YHA accommodation vouchers valid for any hostel and travel by coach, rail and inter-island ferries.
> Armed with a Travel Pass, I intend to explore the system and take part in some of the activities. Exactly what I will write depends on what I find.

From the above example note:

- there is a strong story-line
- it has been suitably researched
- the writer has kept options open.

Sometimes, but not always, it is wise not to be too definite about the content and leave scope for unexpected experiences or angles which present themselves during the trip.

Offering variety

New Zealand offers unlimited scope for articles so, in addition to the above idea, the writer could list several more ideas on different themes. Campervans are extremely popular in New Zealand; that could form the basis of another idea or a sporting theme could be pursued based on activities like white water rafting and so on. It would be relatively easy to put together six or more suggestions.

When you are putting a variety of ideas together, keep in mind the intended readership. If you are writing for young and active backpackers make sure all your ideas are appropriate. In the New Zealand example, youth hostelling is consistent with ideas on sporting activities but the campervan idea would be out of place.

There is no reason why you cannot put another set of ideas together directed at a different sector, one that might prefer to stay in hotels, hire campervans or travel in style and comfort.

Submitting widely

Unlike sending out finished articles, it is very sensible to send your ideas around to various editors at the same time. If two editors happen to like the same idea, it is no problem since the articles themselves can be written quite differently.

Using alternative approaches

Try not to be stereotyped in your presentation. Different ideas might need different treatments and in some cases it might be necessary to give more detail, in other cases less. The technique is to intrigue and make the editor want to learn or read more.

Another approach which can work successfully is to present the opening sentences or paragraph. Often this works well when you have, for example, a humorous style in mind so the opening clearly indicates the style of the article. This worked for an article of ours on the Greek island of Kefalonia.

There was a long silence as we stood in front of bristle face in Argostoli's tourist office. Perhaps he hasn't heard us enter, I wondered, perhaps he has a pea stuck in his ear like the old man in Louis de Bernieres' book *Captain Corelli's Mandolin*. Perhaps all men on this island stick peas down their ears to keep out the sound of nagging wives.

Slowly he raised his head from a prolonged study of a single sheet of paper on his desk. Ash from his cigarette yielded to gravity and filtered down into his woollen jumper adding to the stains of tzatziki and ouzo. 'Parakalo' he muttered, quickly switching to 'yes' when his bleary eyes came to focus on us.

Awaiting a response

Having sent material off to a publisher, either a speculative article or ideas for a commission, expectation tends to run high. Unfortunately, it is a world in which nothing unfolds very quickly so patience must be counselled. It is usually weeks before any sort of reply is obtained and it can be months. After six to eight weeks, it is not unreasonable to raise an enquiry. This can be by phone or by letter. It does not always pay to be too persistent with your follow-up otherwise the editor may simply issue a rejection slip in order to dismiss you.

Receiving a commission

A thin looking envelope through the letter box one morning might easily bring a commission. It is usually short and simple stating the article required, the length and the payment offered. Payment is usually in the form of £s per 1,000 words. Rates vary enormously. Top glossy magazines pay good money, attracting leading professionals. In a sense, the cover charge gives some indication of the rate of pay. The higher the charge the better the rates. National newspapers pay well and tend to be fairly consistent between themselves.

There is a half-way situation where an editor may respond to your ideas simply by asking to see a particular article on spec. This often happens with new writers. It is a promising response. If the article is up to standard there is a good chance that it will be accepted and payment will follow.

WRITING THE ARTICLE

Finding a title

Good, snappy, eye-catching titles can sell an article but it is not always possible to produce them at will. You might well have a title in mind before you start but the best time to worry about the title is when you have finished. Whatever you choose then will reflect the article. If you choose the title first, it is sometimes a struggle to make the article fit. It is like the tail wagging the dog.

Try to avoid hackneyed, overused phrases no matter how appropriate they might seem. On the other hand, if the editor wishes to change the title to 'A Turkish Delight...' or something equally mundane, it will be changed and there's nothing you can do about it.

Structuring

There is a standard piece of advice offered to anyone settling down to write an article whether it concerns travel or anything else – make sure it has:

- a beginning
- a middle
- an end.

It might seem obvious but it is not always followed. Each part of the structure has a function.

Getting started

Just like an appetiser, the beginning serves to catch the reader's attention and makes them want more. Not only does it stir an interest in the reader but it sets the tone of an article and leads naturally into the middle section.

There are no hard and fast guidelines since each and every article is so very different. In travel articles it does help if you can set a mood and a pace so the reader is instantly in touch. The best advice is to read as many travel articles as you can lay your hands on and take particular interest in the opening paragraph. Take note also of those which appeal to you and study the style and content. Here are two very different examples from our own writing offered by way of illustration.

Example 1

Bathed in warm evening sunshine, Mytilene town looked decidedly tranquil from the deck of ferry boat *Romilda* as the ship made ready to dock. The stillness was about to be shattered with the simple act of disembarkation. An unheralded skill of the Greeks is their aptitude for chaos and chaos management which is at its very best at moments of no crisis and can be generated from nothing in travel situations. A very fine exhibition was about to be enacted.

Example 2

Serra da Estrela is Portugal's highest and most admired range of mountains. It is a treasure house of wonders for lovers of the countryside. It acts as a barrier across the country, a point where Mediterranean, Atlantic and Continental influences dramatically converge to shape the character, the land use and the customs of the people.

Reaching the middle

The middle serves up the main course and contains all the information you wish to impart. It develops the promise held out in the opening paragraph and satisfies the reader. Just how much fact you impart in this section depends on the type of article and on the publication.

It has become fashionable in newspapers to separate pure fact out of the body of the article and offer it separately in a box at the end. Desktop publishing programmes allow boxes to be incorporated anywhere on a page, with or without lines, and they have become an important tool for a publisher. Not only does this device allow text to be separated or highlighted, it can also enhance the design layout.

You may be asked to supply text suitable for a box as part of your commission.

Getting to the end

A good, nicely rounded ending is just about as important as a good beginning. Avoid the mistake of providing a summary – the ending should conclude the story-line and bring everything to a satisfying conclusion.

It is less easy to give examples of endings because they lead from the full article and do not necessarily stand alone. Again, the best advice is to read plenty and look particularly at the structure of articles as much as the content.

PRESENTING WORK

Presentation is every bit as important as the article itself. If you take care with the presentation, the editor will know immediately that you have taken the same care with the contents. Hand-written work is unlikely to receive any attention. It is a fact of life. Editors are busy people and if they cannot read something easily and quickly, it will not get read at all.

Word processing

All work should be either typed or printed from a word processor and preferably the latter. There are a number of good reasons:

- it is professional
- it is convenient
- the editor may ask for the disk.

Nothing fancy is called for:

- use plain white paper
- type only on one side
- leave the normal margins, about one inch right and left
- type lines with a double space
- number pages.

Double spacing is easily done on a word processor and can be done when the document is complete. Its purpose is to make life easier for the editor. Editing is still largely done on paper so it leaves plenty of space for pencilled amendments or editorial instructions.

Adding the cover page

To make the whole presentation look especially neat and professional, add a cover page. The information needed for the cover page includes:

- the title
- your name and address
- number of words
- the initials FBSR.

Everything is self-explanatory except perhaps for the initials FBSR. This simply stands for First British Serial Rights and indicates that the article has not been previously published. Note there is no page number.

The title page is a great opportunity to show your skills on the word processor, to use different fonts and point sizes, and your expertise at layout. Figure 9 shows an example.

The covering letter

Whether you are submitting a speculative article or just proposals, you will need a covering letter. It pays to keep it short but there is some information you will need to impart.

The editor wants to know a little about you. Say if you have been published before and perhaps add a copy of an article. Say nothing if you have not been published before but concentrate on your qualifications for writing this particular article. Maybe you have just finished walking a long distance footpath in the Peloponnese or you have some particular involvement with the topic.

Sometimes it is appropriate to briefly summarise the article for the editor or comment on the underlying philosophy. State also if you have photographs to support your articles or proposals and say if they are prints or slides. The letter should not exceed one side of a sheet of paper.

CHECKLIST

- Identify your intended market and readership.

- Plan to write some speculative articles.

- Submit ideas to win commissions.

- Make the presentation of your work look fully professional.

- Keep your accompanying letter short and to the point.

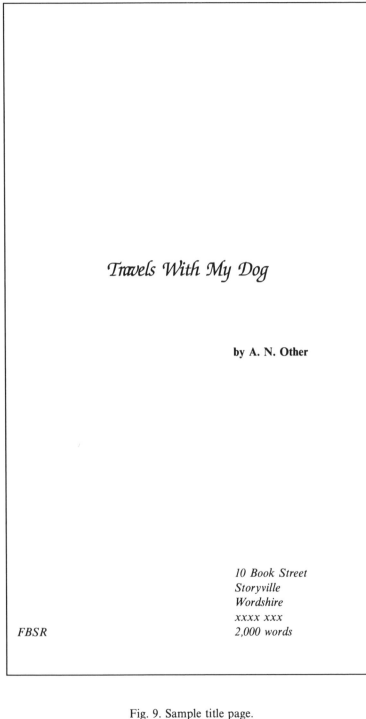

Travels With My Dog

by A. N. Other

10 Book Street
Storyville
Wordshire
xxxx xxx
2,000 words

FBSR

Fig. 9. Sample title page.

CASE STUDIES

Caroline starts work

Caroline has been busy putting together some ideas to try and gain a commission. For the moment she is developing three possibilities:

1. An article entitled 'Kids for Free'. With entrance fees to places of entertainment so high, families cannot always afford to visit as many as they would like. Visitors to Devon are not always aware of the places which admit either families or children without charge.

2. 'Children Friendly Pubs' is the concept behind another idea. It is one which she thinks will have good local appeal. She has a local paper in mind and will ask them to consider it as a monthly feature.

3. Devon is famous for its cream teas and Caroline feels that there is scope here for an article. She would like to link a few of the better known places into a touring article which would incorporate interesting places to visit in the county.

Caroline realises the importance of collecting enough information beforehand to make solid proposals. In fact she feels inclined to draft out each article first so she can write a pertinent summary to submit. From that position she could polish one article to submit on a speculative basis.

Mike and Susan worry about their portfolio

Mike and Susan are busy moving towards submitting proposals for a guidebook. One thing that worries them is, if asked for a portfolio of their work, they have nothing to show but photographs.

They have decided to divide their efforts for a time. Mike plans to write one or two articles on wild flowers, probably starting with the wild orchids of Greece. These articles will be for learned journals and Mike feels confident they will be published. Journals like these do not normally pay subscribers but having a published article is more important.

Susan will try her hand at writing up walks for a local newspaper. Success here will give them a reasonable portfolio to support the type of guidebooks they would like to start writing.

Rob takes advantage

Knowing the importance of having some publications to his name, Rob is keen to take advantage of all the help he can get from his college tutor.

His tutor has explained the two types of approach, either submitting finished articles on spec or just submitting ideas. Rob is keen to try the speculative approach since he knows he will get plenty of help and advice on drafting the article. He has plenty of experience to draw upon from his earlier travels, so he may also circulate some ideas since his tutor strongly favours that approach.

7
Preparing a Guide Synopsis

If you plan to author a new guidebook, you will need at some stage to prepare a synopsis to submit to a publisher. Chapter 8 talks about publishers and it is important to read Chapters 7 and 8 before starting to write your synopsis.

There is an alternative to proposing a new guide. You might be content simply to work on revisions to produce further editions of existing books on a fee-earning basis. All that is required here is to write a letter stating your interest. There is more comment on writing new editions in Chapter 8.

SELECTING IDEAS

One purpose of all the necessary market research is to help with the formulation of an idea or a series of ideas. A temptation to avoid is proposing impulsive projects, something you would dearly love to do, rather than commercial ideas.

A publisher will look at any proposal with one thought uppermost – will it make money for the company? The criteria which you should apply to your own ideas before raising a submission are quite simple. You must ask yourself:

- Will it make money for the publisher?

- Will it make money for the author?

- Is the project achievable?

Considering financial aspects
Making money for the publisher is top of the tree. Any idea which looks set to make money will be received with open arms. If it makes money for the publisher it will also make money for the author, especially if the author is working on a royalty basis rather than on a fixed fee. Unfortunately, it is such a competitive market that even

quality products need considerable promotion to gain a bigger than average market share.

To make money for the publisher, the book must stimulate the buying public either by its usefulness or by its appeal. Visual appeal is a major factor in turning browsers into buyers in the bookshop. Strong colour and good photographs are all part of creating an attractive product.

Ensuring an income
When contracted for a book, an author will be offered either royalty terms or a fixed fee, depending on the publisher. There is no choice involved, it is one or the other. If the author is to make money out of the project, something resembling an income, then the cost of the project must be borne in mind.

With a contract in hand, it may be possible to get some support for the project from the appropriate tourist authority (see Chapter 10). This will not cover all your costs by a long way. Generally, all the expenses usually fall on the author and these are considered in fixing the fee or the royalty advance but they are rarely enough. Always bear in mind the cost when making a proposal and avoid those which appear unduly expensive, at least in the beginning. Achievability must always be kept in mind. With grand, sweeping ideas either the time-scale involved, the cost or your own physical limitations may stand in the way of a satisfactory completion.

Taking the publisher's point of view

A proposal falling onto a publisher's desk is considered not just on the basis of commercial viability, but on how it fits into their publishing list.

If the proposal is for an extension of an existing series, then it will be considered on merit. On the other hand, if it moves the publisher into a slightly new area, no matter how closely related, there could well be some hesitancy. For example, if a publisher already has a travel guide covering the whole of Spain and a proposal lands on the editor's desk for a book covering just the region of Andalucia, it may face rejection on the grounds that it stands in isolation as their only regional guide for Spain. In this case it is better to propose not one title but a short series covering the various regions. This would be looked on more kindly and may result in a contract for a number of titles.

Supposing you felt that a holidaymaker's guide to the history of Greece would be a good idea. A publisher would be unlikely to take it up unless you could extend the idea into a series covering other popular holiday areas. One title on its own gets lost on the bookshelves in a shop but a series catches the eye. If a reader likes one, another purchase might follow. A short series would contain at least six titles.

APPROACHING A PUBLISHER

With an idea in mind or a number of ideas, the problem is that of making an approach to a publisher. Just which publisher to approach is something that is discussed in the next chapter. It must ultimately be done on paper in the form of a synopsis. This is true for all authors not just for new authors. The next section explains the reasons for this.

Book editors, like magazine editors, are busy people but their problems are often less immediate. Mostly, they will talk to new authors on the phone. Sometimes it can pay to make some general enquiries to see if they take on new authors and there might be some feedback on the sort of areas in which they are currently interested. More than likely, if you ask about specific ideas, you will be asked to put them in writing. This means that you will need to prepare a synopsis for each idea and there will be a considerable amount of groundwork required.

STATING YOUR CASE

The object of your synopsis is to explain your idea to the publisher in clear, concise terms but in a whole and complete way. Commercial information may also need to be included in your synopsis. Keep your presentation easy to read. Clear headings logically presented will guide the editor through the synopsis. This is not the time for muddled writing, ideas must be fully crystallised, well presented and easily appreciated. Your future with the publisher depends on this document as much as on your skills and abilities.

Again, look from the publisher's point of view. Apart from the points already discussed, there are other considerations:

- How much competition is there in the market-place for this title?

- What will be the scope of the book?

- How much would the book cost to produce?

- Who would supply the illustrations and maps?

All these questions must be answered or discussed in your synopsis. Editors are far too busy to research every synopsis which falls on their desk and the onus is on the submitter. Failure to present your case clearly with the right information is nothing more than wasted effort.

Choosing your approach

Figure 10 shows an example of a synopsis which has been drafted only for illustration. It has not been thoroughly researched as a serious proposition but it does show the sort of approach needed.

Each synopsis will be necessarily different and will require a different treatment. Some of the headings used in this example may not always be appropriate and different ones will need to be introduced.

The proposal

An editor has to be clear on the nature of the proposal from the very first moment. An unambiguous statement is essential. If it is an additional title to an existing series, for example, say so clearly.

The scope

It is only necessary to define when the book covers a region rather than a whole country or island. When a proposal suggests a new series then it is particularly important to define the scope of each book.

Philosophy

This is only needed when it is necessary to explain the thinking behind the book.

Market situation

A heading such as this is almost always required. It is important to report honestly on the competition the proposed book can expect to find on the bookshelves. This is very much a critical review and you will be expected to stress how the proposed book differs and the advantages it offers.

An editor will take this review at face value initially but should the idea prove of interest, the publishers may conduct their own survey.

Defining the contents of the book

Defining the content of the book takes considerable thought. It is necessary to decide beforehand just what the book will include and how it will be presented.

SYNOPSIS: FUN DAYS OUT IN BRITAIN

Proposal: An entirely new series of illustrated books aimed at people spending their holidays in Britain, including those arriving from other countries.

Scope: Each book will cover a particular region of Britain.

Philosophy: In the short span of a holiday, holidaymakers do not wish to spend too much time finding out where they might go and what they might see. These books will address that problem. Each book will be thoroughly researched to present the best places of entertainment, both indoor and outdoor, in each region. Major centres of entertainment will be presented as a day excursion and will include transport connections and all the necessary details to make the day complete. All a holidaymaker will need to do is thumb through the book to find an excursion which appeals and go and enjoy it. All the detailed planning will have been done for them.

Market situation: This proposed series will be unique in the way it collates and presents information. A number of other titles (quote books) do give information on places of entertainment but not in such a well organised and convenient manner.

BOOK CONTENT

Introduction: Introducing the character and qualities of the region.

Getting around: A section dealing with local transport giving a clear idea of the bus and train services available.

Where to stay: A brief guide to the resorts and towns of character which make a suitable base from which visitors can explore the region.

Days out: Each book will offer a choice of around 20 full or half-day trips to places of entertainment. Places of interest not covered by these excursions will be listed separately with some background information.

Each area will differ in the type of entertainment it has to offer. It is planned to cover:

1. Theme parks, zoos, hands-on museums, cinema complexes.
2. Interesting places, towns, villages, and castles.
3. Areas of natural beauty, parks, waterfalls.
4. Walking and the countryside where this is appropriate.

Length: Each book will run to around 50,000 words.

Illustrations: These will be supplied by the author as 35mm colour slides.

A Day Out at Chester Zoo is written out in detail and included by way of example.

Fig. 10. Example of a synopsis.

If the book in question is a fairly standard type of travel guide covering a whole country, say Spain for example, then some detailed planning is in store. The synopsis for the contents of the guide might look more like Figure 11.

Assessing the book length
The proposer is expected to stipulate the length of the book as a word count. A publisher needs to know exactly the size of book you have in mind. This figure is necessary to work out a costing and it will be included in any subsequent contract awarded to you by that publisher.

For those not already engaged in the industry, quoting a word count is akin to pulling a rabbit from a hat. It is hard to give any firm guidelines since travel guides vary so much in their make up. Overall, a book is made up of words, pictures and maps so a page count does not truly reflect the number of words. The actually page size, font size and line spacing also has a bearing. The following is offered as a rough guide:

- This book contains around 35,000 words.

- A book with 40,000 words, including photographs and maps makes up around 140–150 pages just less than A5 size.

- An A5 book with 80,000 words and pictures makes up to around 200–250 pages.

In other words, 30,000 words makes up to an easily carried guide, not too big, but 80,000 words moves into the realms of a fairly substantial book. Travel guides significantly larger than this are often a compilation of the work of several authors.

FINALISING A SUBMISSION

With all arguments finalised and committed to paper, all that is needed now is to be sure the document is well presented. It should be typed or printed, free of errors and spelling mistakes, crisp and neat in appearance. This in effect is your calling card. All the commissioning editor knows about you at this stage will be learnt from the content and presentation of the synopsis and the accompanying letter. It will give an editor confidence if it is evident that you have taken care, that you have researched the idea well and can present your work logically and clearly. These are the very qualities an editor will be looking for in new authors.

CONTENTS: A TRAVEL GUIDE TO SPAIN

Introduction: This will include comment on the culture, politics, economics, geography, geology, plants, wildlife, environmental issues, sports and pastimes.

History: This will be informative, not too detailed, but adequate to offer a framework to build on in the various chapters.

Food and drink: National dishes and the food that tourists can expect to find on the menu will all be described as well as the popular wines of the country.

Chapter 1: Define here the area to be covered in the chapter and just how it is to be covered. If practical information is to be included, like opening and closing times of places of interest or details of hotels in the region, then the treatment must be explained if it is to be included in the text or listed at the end of the chapter.

Chapter 2: Each and every chapter will be defined in the same terms.

Facts for visitors: There must be a place somewhere for all those necessary facts like visa requirements, emergency telephone numbers *etc*. The editor will need to know how they will be included.

Length: About 80,000 words.

Fig. 11. Defining the contents of a proposed guide.

Title page

It is not expected that your synopsis will run beyond two pages but even so it is worth having a title page. This can be prepared as the example shown in Figure 9 but suitably adjusted. It is inappropriate here to include either the word count or FBSR.

Identifying each page

All pages, except the cover page, should be numbered and carry a strap. A strap is nothing more than a line identifying the author, the work and possibly the page number. It is usually produced in a smaller point size and it sits in the top or bottom corner of the page.

For example, a strap for this book would be simply: *Anderson/How To/Travel/1*.

This is very easily done using a word processor and is usually added on completion. It ensures that should the pages become separated on the editor's desk they are easily identifiable.

Sending off the synopsis

All that remains now is to type up an envelope large enough to take the work without folding and send it off. Remember to include a stamped and addressed envelope for its return. It does not necessarily have to be the same large envelope but one which will take the work folded.

Send it only to one publisher. If you have done your research on publishers (see next chapter) it will have been tailored especially for that publisher anyway. There is nothing to stop you sending more than one synopsis to the same publisher. Nor is there anything to stop you sending different ideas to other publishers. The more ideas you have floating around, the more likely you are to pick up a commission.

ARRIVING AT THE PUBLISHERS

From the moment of posting, there is nothing to do but sit and wait. Waiting requires patience and it can be quite a long wait for one reason or another. We can follow an imaginary synopsis and build up a few scenarios as to what might happen at the publishers.

Receiving a quick response

In smaller firms which have perhaps a limited list, the editor will require only a brief scan of the synopsis to assess a level of interest. If it is inappropriate, a short note thanking you but declining your proposition will be scrawled probably on your original letter and returned instantly.

Smaller publishers tend to respond more quickly mainly because decision-making is in the hands of just one or two people. In addition, they tend not to be so inundated with ideas and proposals. Under these circumstances, a positive reply may not be too long in coming.

Preparing for a slow response

There is a very good chance that the synopsis will be opened by a secretary and simply added to the editor's in-tray. After a cursory glance the editor will transfer it to another tray full of similar proposals, the slush pile.

Landing in the slush pile

Everything in the slush pile does get read eventually but it all depends on the editor's work load. It is usually heavy all the time but worse in some seasons than others. Many travel books are aimed at the spring market so there is often a batch of new titles or editions going through in the preceding months.

In larger firms with several departments, the synopsis may well be circulated around. It moves from editor to editor and can take a month or so to emerge. A follow-up enquiry after six to eight weeks is quite in order either by telephone or by letter.

Costing out an idea

Another reason for a long delay may be because the publishing company has decided to cost out the idea. Based on the information supplied in the synopsis, on the number of chapters and the length, a costing exercise can be undertaken. A consideration will be made for the number of illustrations and maps likely to be required and an overall cost obtained. This gives them a selling price so they can assess how competitive the book will be on the bookshop shelves.

Market research

The company may also ask its sales team to gather a market response to the suggestion. All this means is that enquiries would be made with their retail outlets to see if they could sell such a title.

All this takes time and, more than likely, you will not be informed. A phone call helps in these circumstances since they will often admit that they are considering the idea very carefully.

Ultimately, a letter arrives offering a commission or rejection. Rejection may not necessarily be the end of the road but this is discussed in Chapter 8.

CHECKLIST

• Crystallise your ideas ready to commit to paper.

• Complete all the background research.

• Be confident that your ideas have commercial appeal.

• Develop some persuasive arguments to sell your idea.

• Set about drafting your proposal.

• Make sure it is a professional looking document on completion.

CASE STUDIES

Caroline changes her mind

Caroline had planned originally to become involved only in writing travel articles because of her situation with the children and the lack of time.

She has been working on the idea of featuring tea-shops which are especially renowned for their Devon cream teas, together with places of interest in the locality. The idea is that visitors could tour the locality by car and end up at one of the recommended tea houses. It would create a focal point to a tour.

Now that she has had more time to develop her thoughts, she realises that it would be ideal for a small guidebook. It does not have to be too ambitious, perhaps about 30,000 words, made up into around eight chapters. Since Devon is a popular holiday destination, the book would have a wide market and be very helpful for visitors.

Caroline is satisfied that she could still do the articles as originally intended then build them up into a book. With this in mind she intends to start work on putting together a synopsis. First she must start some market research to check out the competition on the bookshelves and to find a suitable publisher.

Mike and Susan start writing

So far their searches through book titles has revealed nothing which links together walking and flowers. They have become excited by the idea of producing a series of books under a 'Green Guide' title. Each book would describe a number of walks and also identify the flowers found along the route. The Mediterranean islands would be ideal locations.

Carried away with their enthusiasm, they have started to put a synopsis together. It starts: Proposal: Green Guides – a series of guidebooks aimed at an untapped market sector of the travel industry.

In thinking through their idea, Mike and Susan have also stopped to question their motives. It has led to a lengthy debate on whether they are pursuing this idea with enthusiasm only because it would give them enormous satisfaction. Mike argues that it will appeal to two markets, to walkers and to flower lovers. That, he claims, should make it commercially viable. Not wholly convinced, Susan agrees that they should continue with the synopsis for the lessons they will learn from the exercise. In the end, she comments, it is up to them to persuade a publisher.

Rob becomes impatient

Rob is worried about securing work to take up the moment he has finished his writing course. He tutor has warned him that it can take time to secure commissions so he is keen to get started.

He is putting together a synopsis for a guidebook on the Silk Route. His tutor is strongly advising against this at the moment, pointing out that he has not had time to fully research the idea. A poorly argued case is doomed to failure, he points out to Rob, and is a waste of time.

The tutor could only counsel patience and advised Rob to spend time researching suitable publishers first. He reminded Rob of an earlier discussion in which Rob had pointed out that he needed fee-earning work to start his career. A quick way into the profession, he suggested, is to consider offering his services for writing updates and new editions. All that is needed for this, he went on, is to put together a letter and CV and send it around to the larger publishers.

8
Finding a Guide Publisher

Publishing is a large and complex industry, ranging from large multinationals looking towards world markets to small publishers content with local distribution. To add to the complexity, the industry seems to be in a perpetual state of change with take-overs and amalgamations. Apart from the financial health of a company, there is little to concern intending authors on the broader business front.

Much more important is the profile of any particular publisher: the nature and extent of their business, the titles published, the direction in which the publisher is moving and, ultimately, the scope for new authors. A lot of this information will come to light in a piecemeal way during the time spent researching. It is worth collecting it all together and the easiest way is by starting an index, as already suggested in Chapter 4.

DEVELOPING AN INDEX

The UK is not especially short of travel guide publishers. Not all of them are household names by any means. Many of them are quite small and concern themselves only with specialist or local guides. When the numbers are whittled down to those covering a particular field, the list is much smaller so the task of developing your card index (see Figure 12, page 88) or computer file to add more information is not too onerous.

Finding information
The sources of information are basically those already suggested:

- reference books
- bookshelves
- catalogues.

Although you may have already scanned these, there is still more to learn once you are clearer about the project, or indeed projects, you intend to pursue.

Using reference books
The various writers' yearbooks, particularly those already mentioned in Chapter 4, are a natural starting point. Your first step is to select those publishers with an interest in travel. Some of these books have a classified index which can be helpful as long as their limitations are realised. The limitations being:

1.   Publishers often quote 'Travel' in their sphere of interest even when they have only the most tenuous connections.

2.   The index is drawn from the book which itself does not necessarily provide a comprehensive coverage. In other words, not all publishers are listed in the book in the first place.

Scanning bookshelves
Scanning the bookshelves in a good bookshop is still the best way to find out which publishers are active in producing travel guides. Even the best bookshops rarely have a comprehensive selection of travel guides but some of the specialist shops come close. It is surprising how many more publishers have books on the shelves but are not listed in reference books.

Obtaining catalogues
These are an invaluable source of information which reveal rich detail about the publisher's activities. All available books are listed, sometimes with notes on the edition and date of publication. Just as important, the publisher often uses the catalogue to advertise forthcoming new titles and editions. This brings you up to date with the direction in which a publisher is moving and gives clues to current business strategies. Publishers will usually send you a copy of their catalogue free of charge.

Selecting by elimination
Having drawn up a fairly comprehensive list of publishers, the time is right to start taking cards out of the index. From the information gained from all the above sources, you should have a clear idea of the areas of interest of each publisher in your index. Now starts the elimination process.

Matching your own interests against the publishers on file, many cards can be set aside. For example, if you are interested only in producing guides for the UK, publishers which only produce overseas guides can be moved to a different section. Do not dismiss publishers entirely when they are not of immediate interest, they can quite easily change. There are always publishers looking to introduce new series and expand their areas of interest. These are the very publishers who will have commissions to place.

With the elimination complete, the list will be considerably smaller and it is now time to start finding out more about the selected few.

PROFILING A PUBLISHER

Assessing the prospects for work
The information needed about a publisher to assess the prospects for work include:

- annual turnover
- number of new titles published annually
- major series
- new series
- method of paying authors.

Annual turnover
This figure is quoted in some of the reference books already mentioned. It gives an indication of the size of the company. A turnover of £1 million or less represents a relatively small company, £5 million or more and you would be dealing with a relatively large company.

Large and small companies offer different work opportunities. They are discussed separately below.

New titles
This is one of the best indicators of the activity of a company. Allowances must be made for the size of a company – clearly small publishers will produce fewer titles than their larger competitors. New editions are often counted as new titles.

Work prospects are not promising from publishers who have a good list of guidebooks but offer very few new titles or simply offer new editions as new titles.

Major series

Publishers offering one or more major series of travel guide will almost certainly need new authors to help with new editions.

Most contracts for new travel guides include a clause that requires authors to make themselves available for preparing further editions. Equally, contracts have suitable escape clauses which allow the publisher to offer the work elsewhere should the author not be available. There will always be a proportion of authors who are not available for some reason or other. The bigger the series, the more opportunities that will be available.

New series

New series offer great opportunities for work. The secret here is to become aware of them at a very early stage. Catalogues offer the best clue to an emerging series but very often a publisher will have commissioned a good range of titles in advance. Nevertheless, it is a time for prompt action.

Payment

It is always useful to know if a publisher pays royalties or fees. Royalties are paid either annually, half annually or sometimes quarterly. This has to be something to take into consideration when working out cash flows. Accountants would no doubt advance strong arguments for having a good mix of staggered royalty payments with a few fee-paying jobs thrown in. Financial planning on this scale is something of a luxury when starting out into the profession but it may become important later.

Figure 12 offers an example of how to record all the information in a publisher profile.

WORKING FOR A LARGE PUBLISHER

There are many advantages in working for a large publisher:

- greater prospects of work
- the advances or expenses are likely to be better
- the royalties or fees are likely to be higher.

Greater bureaucracy is the downside. When a company is large enough to divide up the functions within the firm into different departments, decision-making can take a very long time. Publishing times too can be longer and the whole time-scale of work drawn out.

Publisher Profile

Company: XYZ plc, address, telephone & fax numbers, e-mail address.

Travel editor: Ms Bloggs, commissioning editor; there are several editors.

Catalogue: Received January 199X. This is the new edition for the current year and has been out since last November. Over 200 titles listed.

Areas of interest: Extensive overseas interest, limited UK interest.

Series titles: Four major series:
XX Traveller covering Mediterranean countries: 54 titles
XY Destinations covering popular Mediterranean destinations: 38 titles
YY World Traveller covering major countries of the world: 65 titles
ZZ City Guides: 32 titles.
UK interest restricted to lifestyle books, hotels, restaurants *etc.* Remaining titles fairly random, some picture books.

Illustrations: All books are well illustrated with colour pictures, typically 60 pictures for the larger books and 40 for smaller guides.

New titles: Some six new titles are advertised for publication in 199X, four in the XY Destinations series. 14 new editions, mostly 2nd, in the YY World Traveller.

Conclusions: The World Traveller has been on the market for some eight years and it is clearly being revamped. Checking on the bookshelves, the cover and style of presentation has changed so there may be work opportunities on this series. XY Destinations is still expanding. Looking through the list there are still some locations not covered, Rhodes and the Peloponnese are two possible titles for Greece, Tuscany and Umbria for Italy and the Lisbon area of Portugal.

Payment: By fee.

Turnover: Around £20 million.

Fig. 12. Sample publisher profile.

If your work meets with approval and you meet the deadlines as requested, there is a real chance of continuity. New projects will be on offer as and when they occur with the flexibility to accommodate your work schedule.

Looking for revision work

There are real prospects of picking up some revision work with large publishers who run one or more series of travel guides. An approach by letter is all that is required. First be sure that you are entirely familiar with the concept of the book or series for which you are offering your services. Your awareness will show through in your letter and give the editor confidence that you can handle the work. Keep your letter short, no more than one page. State your availability, particular areas of interest and experience.

The editor will be in touch and you may be asked to write a sample piece. It is a straightforward test of your writing skills and your ability to adapt to their format. The topic may well be left to you or some broad area indicated. You may or may not be given guidelines but be sure to use the style and format of the book series.

Do not think that new writers alone are singled out for this treatment. Experienced authors are also expected to write test pieces when joining a new publisher. It is no big deal and most competent writers sail through with ease.

WORKING WITH A SMALL PUBLISHER

It can be very different working in a small organisation and there are some important considerations to bear in mind:

- rapid decision-making
- close contact with the editor and support staff
- a greater opportunity for input.

With only the editor and a limited number of people involved in the decision-making, there is often a quick acceptance or rejection of submitted ideas. It is very likely that you will be expected to work directly with the members of staff over the design and layout. Should you become a regular author then your views may well be sought on matters influencing new titles or series.

Monetary rewards are not usually as high as large companies. Royalties are often the preferred method of payment since the publisher will not have to pay out until the sales start flowing. If royalties are paid annually it could be a year or longer before money is paid out. The real downside is the stability of the company. Small companies are much more affected by market pressures or a downturn in sales. This often means that new projects are put on hold and work suddenly dries up. Should a company go to the wall, then your books may be remaindered with a complete loss of income. All royalties will cease and, in the worst case scenario, a year's royalties already earned may be lost.

When working with small publishers, it is unwise to put all your eggs in one basket. It is better to move your skills around and widen your experience rather than stick too long with one publisher.

SUBMITTING A SYNOPSIS

It takes some work to complete all the necessary research and write a synopsis. There are no short cuts – hard work is the only way to success. Ill-conceived ideas, poor research and a sloppy presentation are nothing more than a direct route to the bin. It wastes everybody's time and ensures that any further ideas submitted do not receive a moment's attention.

When your synopsis is ready, take time to polish it up. Make sure that it is crystal clear and that the idea or concept is easily grasped without ambiguity. When all that is done, you are ready to go!

Do not submit the same idea to more than one publisher. There is no harm in submitting more than one idea to a publisher if you feel that they are all of the same standard.

Playing the waiting game

The very worst part is waiting for a response. As has already been mentioned, it will probably come fairly quickly from a small firm but take much longer from a large company. Patience is the only answer. It is not an excuse to stop work. Use the time to keep exploring new possibilities and producing new ideas. The more ideas you can produce, the greater the chance of success.

If your patience is wearing thin after around four to six weeks, it might be worth risking a phone call to the editor. The answer is likely to be a stand off, claiming pressure of work. It might just jog the editor into some sort of action but it really does depend on work flow.

When the response does arrive, it might be a phone call which is usually positive or a letter which might be either acceptance or rejection. Acceptance calls for some sort of minor celebration, even if it is just a quick burst of exuberance, but rejection is harder to take.

Dealing with rejection

There are going to be rejections, many more than acceptances. These should not be taken personally. It is not a rejection of you or your abilities, it is a rejection of your proposal. There are dozens of reasons why it might have been rejected. The idea is right but the timing is wrong, another author is already working on something similar and so on. The list could be endless.

A rejection letter does not necessarily mean the end of the line unless it is a curt dismissal. If the editor has written a letter indicating perhaps that they saw the value of your idea but it did not quite fit their list, there is cause for hope. What a busy editor will not do is carry out research at this stage and modify the idea. Now is the time for a phone call, or better still, a meeting. If you can engage the editor in conversation, it is possible to find out what the difficulties really are with your idea and how it might be modified. Once you get the editor into this more positive approach, you are virtually home and dry.

CHECKLIST

- Establish your broad areas of interest.

- Produce some fresh sounding ideas which make a real contribution to travel and tourism.

- Short list and profile your selected publishers.

- Be sure the selected publishers will be responsive to your ideas.

- Aim your synopsis specifically at a selected publisher.

- Submit only a polished and professional synopsis.

CASE STUDIES

Caroline sharpens up her ideas

Caroline has been busy researching possible publishers for her idea on car tours in Devon combined with cream tea establishments. She feels that it might be best to approach a small local publisher. There has been nothing but disappointment so far. Local publisher often means only local distribution. She found it hard to believe that this could generate much in the way of financial returns and she did not want her work to be simply a labour of love.

Now she has widened the scope of her search, things are looking more promising. She has unearthed a number of publishers, both large and small which specialise in covering the UK. Caroline is intent on finding out more about them and looking at some of the books they produce. She finds that actually getting her hands on a book gives her a much better impression of the series than simply looking at catalogues. With just a glance at the format and presentation, she can work out the intended market. Number of columns per page, paragraph size, sentence length and illustrations speak volumes without reading too much of the text.

Simply doing the research has helped Caroline to sharpen up her ideas and she feels ready to tackle writing and submitting a synopsis.

Mike and Susan finally agree

Although Mike and Susan have been busy writing a synopsis for their Green Guide series, the research has not stopped. They have uncovered a publisher who seems to be entirely concerned with walking guides covering popular Mediterranean destinations. The guides themselves are printed in colour with a good use of photographs and, although they mainly feature walks, they also include car tours. This is exactly the type of book they would like to write.

After pouring over a catalogue, they realise that the series is still in its growth phase and there is a real opportunity for them here. New titles are appearing at the rate of about three a year, steady growth for a small publisher with only 20 titles. Having looked through the book list, they realise that so far the series is confined to island destinations. The next step is to try to work out which holiday islands are still missing from the list.

They both agree that the Greek island of Samos would be ideal. They have visited the island, they know that it offers great potential for walkers and it is not in the catalogue. The next problem is how to make an approach. Mike suggests that they write to the publisher outlining their plans to visit Samos for a lengthy period and offering to write a manuscript. Mike argues that this pre-emptive approach puts no onus or cost on the publisher and is more likely to encourage a positive response. Susan prefers a simple, direct approach pointing out that if Samos is already in the pipeline, they will have burnt their boats. Susan wins the argument.

Rob writes a test piece

Rob has been busy putting together a letter offering his services for updating travel guides. Included with the letter is a short CV briefly covering his educational qualifications but concentrating more on his travel and writing experience. On the advice of his tutor, he has kept both his letter and CV short and to the point.

From his research he was able to list at least six major publishers who already have very large book lists and pay fees rather than royalties. Rob has dispatched his letter to all six publishers simultaneously. Replies have started to arrive. The first two were much the same, they thanked him for his interest in the company and promised to hold his details on file for future reference. A third reply was by telephone directly from the editor. The editor said that they may have some work available shortly and it would be in Asia. If he was interested would he kindly write them a piece of about 1,000 words, on his own travels in the region. They would send him their guidance notes for authors.

His tutor advises him to get one of their guidebooks from the library and study it. He further advises him to follow the style from their guidance notes and make his piece read exactly like their books. Rob is full of hope that he is on his way to his first contract.

9
Securing a Contract

The whole purpose of all the work and effort so far has been directed towards securing a contract to write a particular guide. An offer may come initially by letter or on the phone offering you the chance to write a particular title and broadly outlining the terms.

If you do not like the terms on offer and flatly reject them, the most likely outcome is that negotiations will promptly cease. Your acceptance at this stage is only token. A contract will be sent to you for your approval.

READING YOUR CONTRACT

Virtually all publishing companies have a standard contract. All the editor will do is take a standard contract, fill in the date, title of book, deadline and royalties to be paid and send it off to you. Whatever you do, it is essential that you read it and seek to understand every clause. In most cases the various clauses of an agreement are fairly straightforward. Figure 13 shows the sort of clauses which are usually included in a publishing contract.

NEGOTIATING

Once you have read the details of the standard type of contract, you will realise that there is little scope for negotiation in most cases. There are one or two points to settle.

Deciding upon a deadline
This is something which will be settled in discussion before the contract is actually drafted. Listen to the publisher but do not be pushed into a very early deadline until you have more experience. More than likely, the publisher will take a lead from you. Once you have had some experience, you will have some idea of how many words per week you can write. You will also have an idea of how

Memorandum of Agreement

1. Parties of the agreement. This identifies both parties in the agreement. The term Author is stated specifically to include the Author's executives, administrators and assigns. The Publisher is described in the same broad terms but also includes their successor in business. This comes into play in the event of a take-over.

2. The work. The title of the work commissioned and the length is stated.

3. Licence to publish the work. In this clause the author licenses the publisher the sole and exclusive rights to print and publish the work.

4. Delivery of typescript. This specifies the date by which the typescript is required and gives details of other requirements, number of copies, line spacing etc. It also includes a termination or penalty clause should the author fail to complete on time.

5. Publisher's undertaking. Here the publisher undertakes to publish the work in a reasonable time at their own expense but with suitable escape clauses for unforeseen circumstances.

6. Author's warranty. By this clause, the author warrants to the publisher that the work is original and infringes no other copyright. The author will also be required to indemnify the publisher for any claims against it for copyright infringements.

7. Author asserts right to be named as the author.

8. Copyright line shall be in the name of the author.

9. Copyright protection. Here the publisher gives some undertaking to take legal action to protect the copyright of the work should it become necessary.

10. Control of production. Publisher states rights to have complete control over the production of the book and bear all the expenses. There is usually a paragraph relating to the cost of correcting the proofs. If this is excessive, it can be deducted from royalties.

11. Copyright material. The cost of any copyright material used in the book is charged to the author.

12. Editorial work. If substantial editorial work is required which the author is unable or unwilling to do, then the publisher reserves the right to employ an editor and set fees against royalties.

13. New editions. Sets out conditions for a new edition and includes the author's obligations.

14. Termination of licence. Sets out conditions for terminating the agreement. This is usually when the book is out of print and the publisher does not wish to reprint.

15. Competing works. This effectively bans the author from doing a similar book for a different publisher which would be injurious to sales.

16. Royalty/fee. This sets out how much royalty/fee will be paid and when. It usually covers advances too.

Fig. 13. Typical memorandum of agreement.

long the research phase will take. Putting these together, you will be able to make a sensible and accurate assessment.

Allowing some leeway
The best advice is to leave yourself plenty of leeway with your first few contracts. This allows for the unexpected, like having time off with flu or more work being offered. If you encounter serious problems with meeting the deadline, circumstances outside your control, contact the editor. It is always possible to renegotiate the deadline for crisis situations.

Fixing payment
Not all authors working for a particular publisher are necessarily paid the same. As a new author there is little scope for negotiating higher fees. Try by all means but be prepared to settle for the offer on the table.

Including illustrations
Although these were not specifically mentioned in the sample agreement in Figure 13, they will appear somewhere in the contract. With a good publisher, there will be a separate contract for photographs which stipulates the format, the number which must be submitted and the intended payment. Payment is invariably a fee paid partly on signing the contract and fully on acceptance of the pictures. An additional fee for photographs is often the icing on the cake which can make a project lucrative.

Smaller publishers will simply write a requirement to provide photographs into the contract. It is not unreasonable to ask for some extra payment or expenses to cover the cost of the film or material used.

Producing maps
Again, a requirement to produce maps may also be written into the agreement. Be sure about the publisher's requirements and be careful about copyright infringements. Discuss this fully at the contract stage.

Simple sketch maps may be all that is required but it depends on the treatment given in the book. Sometimes overlay sketches are required. Here the sketch is made on tracing paper overlaying the main map. All the routes used, points of interest and maybe even petrol stations are added.

Establishing a publication date

Make sure that your contract specifies either a publication date or a specific period within which the book will be published. Some publishers are happy to keep their options open on this issue saying that the book will be published 'within a reasonable period'. Insist on something more specific.

RECEIVING PAYMENT

As mentioned earlier, payment is made in one of two ways:

- royalties
- a fixed fee.

Getting royalties

In principle, this is a payment received for every book sold. It might sound like simplicity itself but in practice it turns out to be rather more complicated. Some of the complications include:

1. There is no standard way of calculating royalties. Some publishers offer a percentage of the UK published price for books sold under normal trade terms. Others pay a percentage of the publisher's net receipts.

2. Not all books are sold at normal trade terms, some are sold at 50 per cent discount for which reduced royalties are paid.

3. Reduced royalties are paid on books sold in bulk to the USA or to a foreign-language publisher.

Publisher's net receipts vary according to selling costs. If a publisher sells to retail outlets via a distributor then selling costs can take 70 per cent of the published price. Direct postal sales have minimal selling cost. This is something to clarify with the publisher.

Advances

Advances are usually part of a royalty package. The amount of an advance will depend on a number of factors; the size of the book, the cost of conducting the field work *etc*. Mostly, publishers will only advance an amount which they calculate will be covered by first-year sales. In any case, it will most probably be paid in two or three stages, usually part on signing the contract, part on submitting the manuscript and the remainder on publication.

All the advances will be deducted from your royalties when they eventually start to flow.

Payment

The contract stipulates the accounting date for the payment of royalties. These are usually paid half-annually or annually. They are not paid on the accounting date but some time later, mostly within three months. In the worst case scenario, if a book is published at the beginning of the accounting year, it can be 15 months before money starts to flow your way. Bear in mind too that any advance is clawed back from initial royalties.

Earning a fee

The fee offered by a publisher is not normally open for negotiation. You simply accept it or look elsewhere for work. If it is a leading publisher, the fee will be good enough to attract professional journalists. There may or may not be additional expenses depending largely on the nature of the project.

Expenses are usually paid up front with part of the fee. The remaining fee is paid on submission of the manuscript and publication of the book.

UNDERSTANDING YOUR LEGAL RESPONSIBILITIES

There will be some clauses in the contract which heap legal responsibilities firmly on the head of the author. These are chiefly concerned with:

- obscene or libellous statements
- originality
- infringement of existing copyright.

These are factors publishers feel are the sole responsibility of the author and they rely on openness and honesty in these matters. While no professional journalist sets out to cheat the world, there are always grey areas where suspicion can be aroused. It is easy enough to read something which catches your attention one day, completely forget about it then produce it as an original thought some months later.

Existing copyright

Infringement of existing copyright can cause the most concern. If there is some material already covered by copyright which you would like to use, it may be possible to get permission.

The onus is placed firmly on the author to obtain all necessary permissions. It is a question of writing off to the owners of the copyright and explaining exactly which parts you would like to use. If it is relatively small, or if it acts as an advertisement for the work, permission will be freely given. There will most certainly be a rider insisting on reference to the original source. If the piece of work requested is judged to be adding commercial value to your product, you will be asked for a fee. The author will be expected to pay this fee.

The use of existing copyright work in guidebooks occurs only rarely and it is something that can generally be avoided.

GETTING HELP

If you are not sure whether the contract you have been offered is fair and reasonable, get help. This is easier said than done since most solicitors are not conversant with the world of books.

There are a number of professional organisations around, like the Society of Authors or the Writers' Guild of Great Britain, which offer help and advice on contracts. Unfortunately, you often have to have been published to qualify for membership. The Society of Authors has an Associate membership for authors who have not yet been published but have had a full length manuscript accepted for publication.

The Writers' Guild of Great Britain offers more hope to new writers. A relatively new grade of membership, Candidate membership, has been introduced to cater for serious writers entering the profession. With the offer of a contract on the table, an application for membership would receive serious consideration. There is a membership fee to pay but that needs to be balanced against the cost of legal advice elsewhere. See the Useful Addresses section on how to contact these organisations.

CHECKLIST

- Read your contract clause by clause.

- Get help and advice if you feel it is needed.

- Discuss with the publisher any aspects on which you need clarification.

- Be sure you can meet the deadline.

- Make sure you understand the terms of payment.

- Make sure the publisher enters a publication date or time limit for publication.

- Sign the contract only when everything meets your satisfaction.

CASE STUDIES

Caroline reaches agreement

Caroline managed to find a publisher for the book she had in mind. It is a small publisher but it uses a major distributor. She is satisfied that the book will appear in bookshops throughout the country.

Payment will be by royalties, with an initial advance of £250 on signing the contract and an equal sum on acceptance of the manuscript. She is a bit disappointed at the amount of the advance, but it will easily cover all her expenses for travelling around the region as well as her immediate office needs. Caroline realises too that without the support of her husband or another source of income, she would not have been able to accept such a contract. On the whole she is well pleased and feels it will be a good launch pad to get her new career off the ground.

There is a matter over the contract which is causing her concern and she is busy discussing it with the editor. It had been her plan all along to write each car tour as an article for publication and combine these eventually into a book. A clause in the contract bans her publishing other work which would damage sales. One article, the publisher claims, will be good publicity, but full disclosure of the book's contents would be unacceptable. Finally, they agree on a compromise situation and Caroline asks for it in writing.

Mike and Susan are delighted

Mike and Susan started working on a synopsis for Samos but soon realised that all the books in the series followed a very strict pattern. Instead, they simply sent a letter offering to write a manuscript for Samos in the style of the series.

A cautious reply was received which asked for two things: some tourism statistics for Samos and a write up of any local walk in the style of the book, complete with a map. Armed with some satisfactory tourist figures supplied, after a frustrating delay, by the Greek National Tourist Office and the required write up, Mike and Susan again approached the publisher. Almost by return post a specimen contract came which they studied in detail.

The publisher explained that the publication date was set for next March, almost 15 months hence, so the deadline would be by the end of November. Mike and Susan both thought that this was reasonable timing. Both of them were excited and delighted at the prospects of spending time on Samos to fully explore the island.

Rob is in a whirl

After writing his test piece, Rob had received a call from the editor inviting him to the office for a chat about work. The editor explained he was looking for authors to update three titles, all within Rob's area of interest. Since Rob was the first to be interviewed he had a choice and he promptly chose Vietnam. The conditions of the contract were briefly explained to him and an assurance sought that these were broadly acceptable before the discussion continued.

The editor made several points very strongly to Rob:

1.   The current edition of the book in question requires a significant rewrite which is often more difficult than starting from scratch.

2.   The deadline is totally immutable.

3.   The time allowed for completion of the manuscript is comfortable for regular authors but Rob might find it tight.

4.   A fee will be paid, plus flight expenses and hotel costs for the first week only.

On the subject of the deadline, the editor explained why the company took such a strong line. The whole diary of an edition is fixed the moment the contract is signed: the date it lands on the editor's desk, the date it goes to the printers and the date of publication. Any delay costs the company money. If an author is responsible for any delay, their status will be viewed less favourably.

Rob left with his head in a whirl but with the realisation that he will be working for a very professional company.

10
Organising the Fieldwork

Fieldwork is the most enjoyable part of the task of writing a travel guide. Unfortunately, time spent away from the office costs money. It hardly takes a calculator to work out that the best profit comes from spending the shortest time in the field and completing the job quickly.

There has to be a balance between the time required to do the job away from the office and the money it will earn. Some careful planning is in store before commencing the project.

PLANNING A PROGRAMME

Much time and duplication of effort can be saved by careful planning. No matter what the project, whether it is based at home or abroad, think through the information required. Pretend you are writing one of your chapters and think hard about what you will write and the information you might need.

Producing a working document

It is a very good discipline when starting out to draft a working document. This might list:

- special equipment you might need
- a timetable for fieldwork
- an itinerary
- a timetable for writing.

Listing special equipment

When working at home, you can usually pick up most pieces of equipment you might need as you go. It is different when travelling abroad. In most cases it is important and some cases vital to buy your preferred photographic film in advance. Similarly if you require a rucksack, compass and notebooks make sure they are all on the list.

Allocating time for fieldwork

It is important to assess the time required to complete this stage. It is difficult to do so without experience. One way is to decide on the total time you can spare, say four weeks, then divide this up according to the places you must visit. Remember, you will not be on holiday but working. It is surprising just how much information can be collected in a 12-hour day.

Planning the itinerary

If the project will keep you on the move, plan your itinerary in advance. Make a diary and decide how many days you will require for each location. Plan every move in advance so you will cover the region in a sensible order. If you are hoping to get help from a National Tourist Office, they will need this information. It is wise to leave a copy of your itinerary with your family or a friend.

Organising your writing

A similar discipline is necessary when the time comes for writing. Decide how long it will take you to write a chapter and scale this up by the number of chapters. Allow some extra time for printing out, reading and reprinting corrected work.

It is very likely that the writing will take longer than you expect. It is hard to give any guidelines since people write at different speeds. That apart, if you are writing largely from memory it is much quicker than when you are constantly referring to notes or stopping to check facts. A short book full of facts can often take longer than a much bigger book.

OBTAINING SUPPORT

Once you are armed with a contract and have taken the trouble to work out a detailed programme or itinerary, now is the time to seek help.

If you are travelling to another country and the publisher is not paying expenses, then it is worth an enquiry at the National Tourist Office of that country. Phone in the first instance and make contact with the Press or Public Relations Officer. You will be asked to put your request in writing, but at least you will be able to ensure that it goes to the right person.

Tipping the scales

Help is by no means assured. If tourism in that particular country is in a slump, the chances of getting help are much brighter. Budgets are increased in these circumstances and there is a greater willingness to help journalists. The converse is also true. When tourism is riding high, the inclination is only to help journalists who work for leading national newspapers. If you can pick up a newspaper commission in addition to your book, there is an excellent chance of getting help. This is exactly how a professional journalist would proceed.

The second most important thing you can do to help yourself is to provide a detailed itinerary. This allows the tourist office to contact possible hotels along the route to see if they can help for those particular dates. With luck you may be offered free accommodation or at least at half price. If you have presented a good case, you may end up with free flights, some accommodation and possibly a car for a short time. Equally, you might come away with no help whatsoever.

DOING BACKGROUND RESEARCH

Finding out as much as you can about your project before you start can save both time and embarrassment. You need to find out exactly what there is to be seen and explored before you go. It is too late after your trip.

The simplest way to do this type of research is to lay your hands on every guidebook available. It is not intended that you should copy from any of them but it pays to be aware of the ground they have covered. It helps you to be aware of new developments in a country, a new theme park or golf course, which is not included in other guides. This way you can ensure that your guide is both comprehensive and up to date.

Writing a little light history

It is very likely that your guide will need some historical background. History is covered in two ways:

1. relating to the social and political development of the country or island

2. as background to an important site or location.

If it is at all possible to write the general history of the country before you go, it will bring enormous benefits to your fieldwork. It helps to put the things you find and see, social behaviour and local customs, into a context which would have been lost on you otherwise. Suddenly you will find interpretative powers you did not realise you possessed.

In a similar way, when you visit a particular location with its own history, you can place this more easily into a general context. Your comments and views then become much more meaningful and helpful to others.

Checking the fact file

There is a lot of information which comes under this category, such as currency, where to change money, bank opening hours *etc*. If you make a comprehensive list before you go it becomes a simple matter to check through the information you need whilst you are there.

WORKING ON LOCATION

This is where all your prior planning and preparation helps you to work efficiently. Forget dreams of days on the beach. On most trips you will be lucky to get even half a day. What you really must do above all else is concentrate on gathering all the information you are likely to need, and more!

Getting help

Help in any form is useful when gathering information. Talking to local holidaymakers can be helpful. Encourage them to advise you of the most interesting things to see in the locality, the best beaches and where to go.

Local tourist offices

Whenever you reach a new town or resort, head for the nearest tourist office. Pick up every leaflet in sight by all means but also announce yourself as a journalist. Sometimes this results in extra leaflets or directories appearing which are intended for those in the trade.

Keeping notes

When you are on location, it is vital to keep good notes. Just how you do this is up to you. A compact hand recorder, the type often seen in the hands of reporters on television, is a must.

It is especially useful when driving around and you need to record some commentary. It will be necessary to transcribe everything on tape on to paper. There is no way you can hope simply to store the tapes until you get home. You could easily end up with more than 100 hours to check through on 50 tapes. It would never get done. What horror if the tapes were damaged in transit or some were lost!

There is no real alternative but to listen to the tapes regularly and condense your notes on to paper.

Making a diary
One way to keep notes is in a diary form. Date each entry in sequence then list your notes for the day. Start an index at the back of the book in the form of locations. Should you revisit a location again at a later date, you can enter that page number against the location in the index.

It matters little which way you keep notes provided that they are:

- systematic
- easily accessible.

Deciding what to note
If in doubt, make some notes. It is almost impossible to make too many notes while on location. A frequent error made by inexperienced writers is to make too few notes.

When you finally start to write the guide, the book often takes on a life of its own. You are led into areas you failed to anticipate and are suddenly let down while in full flow because your notes are inadequate. It can be very frustrating. No matter how many notes you think you need, take more!

Opening hours
Always record opening hours. Whether it is a museum, ancient site, the bank or shops, get into the habit of recording opening hours.

Hotels and accommodation
These usually have some place in a guidebook so you will need lots of information. You might well be able to pick up a directory of hotels at the tourist office. Otherwise, it may mean a visit to each hotel to pick up a brochure which can be very time-consuming.

Restaurants and eating places
It is impossible to try them all but take notes on all you can. Listen to people's recommendations and ask what sort of meal they had and at what price.

Recording first impressions
First impressions are one of the strange phenomena of this world. It is only partly true to say you only have them once. There are some

that never go away. There are some places which stimulate the same thoughts or reaction whenever you revisit. The tall buildings in Lisbon with the tiled façades is a case in point, although not everyone will react in the same manner.

Whatever your first impressions it pays to note them down before they are replaced by further events. They are good to share. Readers feel some empathy with your book and with you as a person if they respond in the same way.

MAKING A CHECKLIST

Whenever there is a need to collect a great deal of information, make a checklist. All that needs to be done then is to fill in all the required details. A systematic approach means that you are less likely to overlook some of the details. You can customise your list to fit any set of circumstances. Figure 14 shows how a completed checklist for beaches might look.

Beach Checklist

Location: close to the resort centre.

Ease of access: steep steps (40) lead down to the beach. No wheelchair access, difficult for families with prams.

Dimensions: approx. 30m long by 10m wide.

Texture: fine sand, fairly uniform.

Colour: bright golden.

Facilities: sun loungers and shades available. Few other facilities because of poor access. Drinks, snacks and food freely available on promenade behind. Two very well situated restaurants on cliff top looking down onto beach.

Sea character: shallow initially, fairly sheltered by cliffs.

Swimming conditions: normally fairly good, a flag warning system in operation.

Water sports: limited to wind surfing and pedalos.

Suitability for children: apart from access, very good with safe paddling.

General comments: attractive setting and picturesque. Generally popular, overcrowded in peak season.

Fig. 14. Making a checklist.

Once you have devised a checklist and found it useful, you can keep it for all time. Any compilation of facts and opinions which needs to be done repeatedly can be treated in the same way.

WORKING ON A LAPTOP COMPUTER

On the face of it, taking a laptop so that you can get on with the writing seems like a great idea. In reality, there is seldom the time.

Much depends on the type of book. If you need to visit places gathering impressions and taking notes, then that alone will take most of the day. If you have been using a tape recorder, the evenings may well be spent transcribing the tape. A laptop becomes especially useful in periods of poor weather when your outside work is restricted or on long journeys. Very often, it is not until you have completed the whole experience that you can start to shape up the presentation of the book. When there are lots of facts to log or if you are also writing articles while you are away, a laptop is invaluable.

CHECKLIST

- Plan a detailed programme for your journey.

- Make sure that you allow enough time to collect all the information you need.

- Prepare as much of the background as possible in advance of your trip.

- Check all the equipment you will need.

- Plan carefully to use your time efficiently out on location.

CASE STUDIES

Caroline feels unsettled

Caroline is disturbed that she is getting little in the way of guidelines from the publisher. The book she has proposed is very much a one-off and does not fit in to any particular series. Although she raised this in discussion, it seems that the editor is happy to leave the style and presentation to her. The only restriction is that she stays close to the structure detailed in her synopsis. Costings have been done on the number of chapters and word length that she quoted and are acceptable.

This lack of direction is leaving her feeling a little unsettled about the project. Her husband has suggested that she goes ahead with gathering information and writing the first chapter. After that she may have a much clearer idea of how to set about the task. At that stage she can work out a more detailed schedule and have more idea of how to tackle the job. Caroline is inclined to agree with her husband on this occasion and decides to follow his advice.

Mike and Susan are taken aback

Mike and Susan have received instructions on the publisher's requirements for their walking book. These are standard, printed instructions given to all authors. They are amazed to find how demanding they are. The instructions explain:

- at least 20 main full-day walks are required
- each walk must have at least two shortened versions
- each walk must be done at least twice
- at least four car tours must be described.

When Mike and Susan settle down to work out the time required, the calculation is quite simple. If each of the 20 major walks are down twice it works out at 40 days. Add a further few days for finding shorter walks plus four days for car tours plus a few days for bad weather. The answer comes as a shock, at least eight weeks! They had no idea it would take quite so long but have decided to stretch it to ten weeks to be on the safe side.

Apart from getting their equipment together, there is little they can do in advance except try to find a suitable walking map.

Rob's in heaven

Rob is still walking on cloud nine and even the arrival of a massive style manual has not brought him down to earth.   The manual details just about every requirement for writing a book in the series. Rob can hardly stop dipping into the book and it is providing a serious distraction from the completion of his writing course.

He is starting to appreciate the preparation he needs to make in advance and how much time good organisation before departure can save. Even though he plans to take a laptop computer, the style manual advocates the use of a small hand recorder which he decides he must buy. Another piece of advice is not to be parted from his work notes while travelling and that they should stay in his hand luggage. His photographic equipment and all the vital tools of his trade should be treated similarly.

With his tickets already booked, Rob can hardly wait to get started.

11
Preparing a Manuscript

When all the fieldwork is done, when all the notes are gathered, it is time to write. Unless you are working on something entirely new, there is a fair chance that the publisher will have some very specific guidance.

WORKING TO GUIDELINES

A copy of the guidelines in whatever form they take will be supplied to you on signing the contract. They may be anything from a few sheets of paper to a rather grand style manual. Generally, notes for authors set out to provide a framework for the series so that each title conforms in style and content.

Following house style

Instructions on house style are usually very specific. They will inform when to use capitals, how to deal with distances, yards and/ or metres, miles and/or kilometres, when to abbreviate, when to hyphenate, preferred spellings and so on. This brings a measure of consistency to submissions from various authors. Following these instructions to the letter will save the editor time and effort and keep you on the preferred list when new commissions are handed out.

Do's and don'ts

There will be plenty of advice on things you may or may not do. The treatment of numerals often causes problems. Small numbers, usually below ten, are spelt out in full while higher numbers appear as figures. 'Do not' is usually preferred to 'don't' but 'it's' is sometimes accepted as an abbreviation. The publisher's requirements in the use of capital letters will be spelt out. Middle Ages may require capitals, for example, but not medieval; France but not french windows – the list can be surprisingly long.

Writing style

There will be clear instruction on whether the style of the book is personal or impersonal. For the style most commonly used in guidebooks the instruction to authors would be:

- Do not write in the first person. Avoid I's and We's totally. These are not to be used in any circumstances.

- The use of 'You' is permitted but its overuse should be avoided.

Sometimes the author is asked to write in an almost totally impersonal style avoiding not just the use of 'You' but also the third person 'He' and 'She'. Avoiding pronouns for the third person cuts out any sexism. Fortunately, the use of 'It' is not usually banned.

Planning the book contents

When putting forward a proposal to a publisher for a new title in an existing series, the written submission will in effect cover the variable part of the book, the main chapters. All the rest of the book will follow precise instructions. Figure 15 shows how author's instructions might look for the introduction section of a guidebook to a country.

In a similar way to the example shown in Figure 15, instructions will clearly detail the publisher's expectations for each section of the book.

WORKING ON COMPUTERS

Most publishers ask for manuscripts to be supplied both on a computer disk and as hard copy. Instructions for electronic formats will be included in the notes supplied to authors. The points covered are:

1. *Treatment of text.* Generally, publishers require just plain text. This means no bold, no underlining, no italics and only initial capital letters as and when required.

2. *Formatting.* Again the requirements are very simple, basically no formatting. Paragraph indentation is not required and the line spacing between paragraphs will be indicated.

Notes for Authors: Introduction

Try to follow the headings listed below and in the same order. Please note that the points mentioned below each subheading are suggestions only. Some may not apply, others might be more appropriate.

Subheadings as follows:

Welcome to...
Outline briefly what makes the country attractive to tourists. Highlight major landmarks and points of interest.

History
An in-depth account of the country's history from prehistoric times. This is a major section and should be given full treatment. Divide the section into appropriate headings, *eg* Roman Times, Middle Ages *etc.*

Geography
A brief account of the geography and geology. Be sure to include major features, *eg* mountains or rivers which influence life in the region.

People
A detailed account of the cultural and ethnic components of the population. Include their beliefs, traditions and social structure. Discuss religious doctrines where necessary but especially where there are religious customs which affect visitors.

Politics and economy
This is nothing more than a brief overview.

Arts and crafts
Discuss all aspects of local crafts including whatever is appropriate, *eg* pottery, jewellery, sculpture, painting, weaving, highlighting particular specialities.

Fig. 15. Instruction notes for authors.

National holidays
Detail important national holidays, especially those which may affect visitors.

Religious and folk festivals
Highlight all major festivals of interest to visitors and discuss their relevance to local culture.

Language
Provide an overview of the language and conclude with a selection of useful greetings and phrases. This will include a basic pronunciation guide to the listed vocabulary.

Flora and fauna
Talk about the flora and fauna in specific terms. Mention plants and animals which are rare, unusual or important to the country. Divide this section into two if needed.

Sports and pastimes
Include national sports important to the culture as well as sports in which the visitor can participate. No specifics of the latter are required here. Details will be listed in the Factfile section.

Food and drink
This will be a major section. Provide an overview of all the national and regional cuisine in the country. Include details on the style of cooking, ingredients, spices used *etc*. List and explain the dishes typically found on the menu. Indicate general meal times, any particular eating habits, *eg* shared dishes, half portions, and dishes to avoid. Comment on tipping.
  Discuss attitudes to alcohol and the types of alcoholic drinks available. Beer and wine might benefit from detailed comment. Talk also about soft drinks and mention any specialities. Describe the situation with drinking water.

Fig. 15. (Continued)

3.   *Preparing the disk*. Most authors work on IBM compatible computers, most publishers use Apple Macintosh. These systems are basically incompatible but certain electronic formats can be transferred from one to the other. It makes the task much simpler if the hidden commands which are used in a particular word processing programme are kept to a minimum. These commands are the ones which control formatting, hence the instruction not to format.

Modern word processing programmes will allow work to be saved in files compatible with alternative word processing programmes. The publisher will specify in which form the work is required. It is likely to be in ASCII files or Rich Text Format (RTF).

ORGANISING MATERIAL

If you have done a thorough job out on location, you should have masses of information. In addition to your own notes, there will probably be a mountain of printed leaflets and booklets. Time spent before starting to write in sorting out this material and organising it to fit your work pattern will pay rich dividends. The simplest approach is to:

• Start a storage file for each chapter of the book.

• Sort through all leaflets and booklets and add to the appropriate file.

• Add a cross reference for material which may be required for more than one chapter.

• Divide up your own photographs in a similar way. Pictures are useful for stimulating your memory when you start to write.

WRITING THE MANUSCRIPT

Getting started

Allow plenty of time when you start writing. The start is always the slowest stage. It takes a little time to develop a structure in your mind which will carry you along without thinking. If there are false starts when the words do not flow, it is generally because you have not settled into an approach consistent with your own style and the requirements of the chapter. It will come with application and some thought. Once you feel happy, the words will start to flow and the momentum gained here will carry you forward into the main body of the book.

Saving time

The best way to save time is to treat the writing as a full-time job. This means keeping up a steady application and avoiding breaks of more than a day or two.

Once you have established a flow, you can mentally tune in to the exact point after a short break. You can remember exactly the pattern of the chapter, what you have already written and the direction you intend to go. After a long break, all that fades from the mind. It takes time to pick up your work again. Time is wasted reading back to remind yourself of where you are up to and how you intended to continue. If the breaks are too long, the whole structure of the book fades from the mind and the flow becomes discontinuous. It may in the end show in your work.

Planning a timetable

This is very hard to do until you come to terms with:

- your own application
- the rate at which you write.

People write at different speeds and some books are quicker to write than others. Guidebooks are often not especially easy to write since there is often a need to break off to check facts. Spelling of foreign place names and a hundred other minor but important details must all be recorded accurately – they are the very essence of a good guide.

Making assumptions

To work out just how long a book might take to write, it may be necessary to make some assumptions initially. Later, when you get down to writing, you can revise your assumptions. Start with the assumption that you can write at about six thousand words a week. Two comments on this assumption:

1. It is a good rate of work for a new writer.

2. The early part of the book will be the slowest, the last part the quickest.

Assume next that the book requires 60,000 words. Then there is ten weeks writing in store. Add more time for reading, correcting and printing. Add yet more time for organising and captioning photographs and maps. In all, around three months must be set aside to complete the work. Much longer will be required if there is any break in continuity.

TIDYING UP FOR SUBMISSION

The great day eventually arrives when all the writing is finished. There are always a few final jobs:

- make sure all pages are numbered consecutively
- add a strap to each page to identify you and the work
- identify maps by chapter and make sure each has a key
- organise pictures by chapters and supply a separate list of captions
- print out pages with a double line space
- prepare a disk which is identical to the printout
- make a clear title page.

Page numbering
The easiest way to work on a computer is to treat each chapter as a distinct file. Finally, it will be necessary to look into each file to see how many pages it runs to. Use the next consecutive number to start the next chapter. If, for example, the first chapter contains eight pages then open the file for chapter two and number the first page as nine. Word processing programmes usually have the facility to start numbering according to instruction.

The final check
Make sure everything is in good order before it is finally submitted. If you have to make any last minute changes, be sure to make them on both the disk and the printout. Do not be tempted to alter the disk without printing out the affected part.

You understand how all the bits and pieces, the manuscript, maps and photographs fit together, the editor does not. Make sure everything is clearly labelled and make it as easy as possible for the editor to get an overview. If necessary make a list of everything that is included in the parcel you send and keep a copy for yourself.

READING THE PROOFS

One day a parcel will arrive containing the proofs. These you will be expected to read and return within a reasonable period, perhaps one or two weeks. The time allowed for this is often stipulated in the contract.

There are lots of editorial signs and symbols relating to proof reading. Each has a very specific meaning. It is useful shorthand for those in the business but it is not essential for authors. As long as the corrections or changes you wish to make are crystal clear, that is all that is required. It is useful to put a couple of lines in the margin opposite to where you make a change or correction just to draw attention to it.

It takes long enough to read a book but it takes even longer when you need to read every word. Make sure you set aside enough time. It is your book and, at the end of the day, any mistakes appearing in the printed form reflect on the author as well as the publisher.

REACHING PUBLICATION

A date for publication will have been set in advance by the publisher. This date allows for the book to get into circulation and out to the shops. It is very likely you will be sent an advance copy some weeks before official publication.

It is a great moment of satisfaction when you actually lay your hands on the finished product. A lot of work, a lot of planning and a lot of yourself has gone into the writing of that book. This is time for a quiet moment of self-congratulation. Others might be pleased for you but nobody can really share your elation unless, of course, you have a co-author.

There are just one or two things remaining to be done.

Registering for public lending rights

Books borrowed from the library qualify the author for a payment. First of all, it is necessary to register your title. There are certain requirements to be met, the author/s must be named on the title page or be able to prove authorship by some other means. Authors must also be resident in the UK or in Germany to qualify. The UK in this instance excludes the Isle of Man and the Channel Islands.

Payment is made based on the number of loans. Sample points are arranged in all regions, and the libraries involved do change from year to year. From the statistics gathered from the sample libraries, the loans are rescaled to arrive at a national figure. Payment is made on this figure. There is a cut off at £6,000 but few authors are affected by this. Available statistics show the majority of authors receive between £1 and £99. An application form and full details of the scheme can be obtained from the office of the Public Lending Rights, the address is listed under Useful Addresses.

Generating some publicity

There is often no harm in seeking a little local publicity. It might help to raise your profile and bring in more work. Contact the local paper, they might run a short piece about you and the book. Contact also the local radio, you might be invited to chat on air about your book and your experiences while researching.

CHECKLIST

- Take time to read your guide notes thoroughly.

- Make sure you understand all the details of the house style.

- Take time to organise your material before starting to write.

- Work out a timetable for writing your book and stick to it.

- Check and re-check your finished manuscript for errors.

- Set aside some time for reading and correcting the proofs.

- Register your book for Public Lending Rights.

CASE STUDIES

Caroline works hard for little

Caroline found writing the guidebook hard work. It was far more time-consuming than she had ever imagined and fitting it into her family life was very difficult. Even when she thought she had finished, there was still much to do in tidying up before submission and again in the proof reading.

She has been working out possible financial returns. The publisher has printed 3,000 copies. Knowing the rate of royalty payment and armed with details of the net income to the publisher, she realises it is possible to work out a maximum return. Assuming all copies are sold through normal trade outlets, the final calculated figure represents a very poor return for the effort she has put into it.

The book will only really pay if good sales prompt further

reprints but only time will tell. She is pleased and proud of the book and glad to list it on her CV. In future, Caroline decides that writing articles will fit more easily into her lifestyle and promises to be much more rewarding.

Mike and Susan take a cautious line

Mike and Susan enjoyed the task of researching and writing their book. They felt it had been a thoroughly enriching personal experience. The cost of the exercise had taken them back a little. Fortunately, the series they contributed to has a long shelf life. It is published in at least three languages and many of the titles are reprinted almost annually. They are confident the book will pay well in the long term. The publisher has commented on their highly professional approach and indicated that there might be more titles on offer for them.

They are pleased to have succeeded but are a little cautious. The way ahead, they have decided, is to take on some fee-paying commissions to provide ready income. This income can then be used to finance further titles in the series on which they are currently engaged. With this balance of work, they can cover their expenses and expect to benefit from increasing royalty cheques in the future.

Rob feels satisfied

Rob found the work extremely demanding but very rewarding. It had been hard work to keep up with the timetable demanded by the publisher. Just reading the style manual had taken up a lot of time and had slowed him down. If he manages to get another contract with this publisher, and the omens are good, he knows he can be a lot quicker.

He feels there is a good living to be made provided that finding new work is not a problem. His photography could also be a further source of income. The next stage, he decides, is to make contact with a suitable slide library which will sell them for him on a commission basis.

All his travel experiences will provide ideal material for writing articles which is another area he intends to develop. All in all, he is well pleased with the start he has made and is determined to forge ahead and build a career.

Glossary

APS. The Advanced Photographic System is a relatively recent development aimed at improving instamatic cameras. It is designed to make using a camera easier and more foolproof. The film, for example, is self loading and only requires the film cassette to be inserted into the camera.

ASCII. A type of file used to store a document on a disk. This file contains only plain text from a document. All other codes controlling layout and special effects are removed. This allows the files to be read into virtually any other programme on any computer. ASCII is an acronym for American standard code for information exchange.

Assignee. A legal term meaning a person to whom rights are assigned.

Autofocus. With reference to cameras, it is a means by which the subject is automatically brought into focus when a camera is operated.

By-line. A line giving credit to the author of a piece of work.

Commissioning editor. An editor empowered to offer contracts to authors for new work.

Desktop publishing. A computer programme which enables page spreads to be designed suitable for publication, as in a book.

Double spacing. Refers to the space between lines on a piece of type or printed work.

Editor. A person who prepares text for publication by checking and improving its accuracy *etc.*

E-mail. Short for electronic mail, this mailing system is available only to those on the Internet. It allows mail or articles to be sent down the telephone line to anywhere in the world for the cost of a local telephone call.

FBSR. Stands for First British Serial Rights and applies to a piece of written work offered for sale for the first time. It is generally assumed that an article not carrying these initials has been previously published.

Font. Used in printing to mean typeface. Fonts can be scaled larger or smaller, see point size.

Grey card. Available from photographic suppliers and used by photographers to measure exposures more accurately.

Internet. The Internet is millions of computers interconnected via a global network. It offers a huge searchable library available 24 hours a day and a method of communication to others connected to the Internet by e-mail.

Modem. A device connected to a computer, either internally or externally, which allows electronic signals to be sent down a telephone line.

On spec. A term used in journalism referring to articles written speculatively rather than by prior agreement.

Point size. Used in printing to refer to the height of a font. A point equals 1/72 of an inch.

This font is in 12 point. This font is in 16 point.

Publisher. A company or person involved in publishing books, magazines or music.

Rich text format. This is another type of file for storing a document electronically on disk. It stores the document with the minimum of codes controlling the format and special effects, like bold and italics. This allows the files to be read more easily into a different word processing programme.

Scanner. A device which allows text documents or graphics to be scanned and converted into an electronic format suitable for a computer.

Search engine. A device which facilitates searching for information on the Internet.

Service provider. A company offering a connection to the Internet with the use of its search facilities on a commercial basis.

SLR. Used in the photographic world to refer to single lens reflex cameras. These offer the advantage of more accurate picture framing since the same lens is used for the viewfinder and for taking the picture. A further facility on most SLR cameras is that the lens can be removed and replaced with another more appropriate lens when the occasion demands.

Slush pile. This is a slang term used by editors and throughout the trade relating to unsolicited manuscripts and articles which pile up awaiting attention.

Strap. Refers in journalism to a line on each page of a piece of work identifying the author and the work.

Word processor. This may be a dedicated machine which facilitates written work offering a range of facilities for handling text, *ie* in moving text into a different place, deleting, restoring, changing the font or point size *etc*. Alternatively, it may be a programme for use on a computer which allows the computer to behave as a word processor.

Useful Addresses

Public Lending Rights, PLR Office, Bayheath House, Prince Regent Street, Stockton-on-Tees TS18 1DF. Tel: (01642) 604699. Fax: (01642) 615641.

The Society of Authors, 84 Drayton Gardens, London SW10 9SB. Tel: (0171) 373 6642. The society offers two grades of membership. Full membership for those who have had a full-length work published, broadcast or performed commercially in the UK. Associate membership for those who have had a full-length work accepted for publication but not yet published and for those authors who have had occasional items broadcast or performed commerically. Both grades pay the same subscription and enjoy the same benefits.

The Writer's Guild of Great Britain, 430 Edgware Road, London W2 1EH. Tel: (0171) 723 8074. Membership is by a points system. A full-length book, an hour-long television or radio play, a feature film *etc* entitles the author to full membership. Lesser work earns Associate Membership status and helps to accumulate enough points for full membership. Previously unpublished writers can apply for membership when they receive their first contract. There is a new grade of Candidate Membership for those taking their first steps in writing but who have not yet received a contract.

Further Reading

Copyright & Law for Writers, Helen Shay (How To Books, 1996).

Creative Writing, Adèle Ramet (How To Books, 1997).

Hart's Rules for Compositors and Readers at the University Press Oxford (Oxford University Press). Packed with useful information for putting words into print, deals with spellings, abbreviations, using capitals. It sets rules for just about every situation encountered by authors and editors.

Photographer's Market (Writer's Digest Books, published by F & W Publications). Revised annually. This book covers trade and consumer magazines and stock photo agencies in the USA. Useful if you plan to sell your work in a wider market.

Starting to Write, Marina and Deborah Oliver (How to Books, 1997).

The Freelance Photographer's Market Handbook (BFP Books). Revised annually, new editions usually available on October 1st.

The Writer's Handbook (Macmillan). Revised annually. New editions reach the bookshelves around September for the following year.

Writers' and Artists' Yearbook (A & C Black). Revised annually. New editions reach the bookshelves around September for the following year.

Writing a Non-fiction Book, Norman Toulson (How To Books, 1997).

Writing for Publication, Chriss McCallum (How To Books, 4th edition, 1997).

Index

COPYRIGHT & LAW FOR WRITERS
How to protect yourself and your creative work

Helen Shay

This book will be a useful tool for any writer, but especially invaluable for beginners and those just starting to enjoy some success. Make sure you never receive any legal short change. This book takes you through the main legal implications relevant to writers, from first putting pen to paper/finger to keyboard through to selling work, entering a contract and onto collecting the full financial rewards due to you. It also explains exactly what to do if things go wrong. It explains the various pitfalls and how to steer clear of them – for example – copyright infringement – whilst showing how to preserve your own rights, and how to publish and not be damned. A graduate of Manchester University, Helen Shay is a qualified solicitor of fourteen years' standing. She has tutored and lectured part-time in business law. She is a member of the Society of Women Writers and Journalists and the Women Writers Network, and currently writes a regular legal column for *Writers News*.

96pp. illus. 1 85703 416 3.

WRITING FOR PUBLICATION
How to sell your work and succeed as a writer

Chriss McCallum

Absorbing and highly informative, this is the fourth edition of Chriss McCallum's popular handbook. No author seriously interested in getting published can afford to be without this book. 'Handy for both professional and newcomer alike.' *Writers News*. 'Excellent.' *Competitors Journal*. Really definitive... Leaves every other similar book in its shade.' *Pause (National Poetry Foundation)*. Chriss McCallum has many years' experience as a professional editor, working for several leading publishers. She was publisher of *The Writer's Voice* (1983–86), is a Member of the Society of Authors, The Society of Women Writers and Journalists, and an Honorary Member of the Comedy Writers' Association. She is co-editor of *Writer's Bulletin*, the markets and resources newsletter.

192pp illus. 1 85703 226 8. 4th edition.

MAKING MONEY FROM WRITING
How to become a freelance writer

Carole Baldock

Would you like to make money from writing, whether poetry, prose or non-fiction? This book will show you how to take responsibility for the business side of your writing right from the start: how to market yourself, how to network and make the most of contacts and opportunities, and how to handle your finances. This step-by-step guide reveals some of the many freelance opportunities open for aspiring writers, and helps you make progress from your initial scribbled jottings to published work of all kinds. After only four years, working as a freelance writer has become a full-time career for Carole Baldock. She is Books Editor for a number of magazines, and contributes to the *Children's Britannica*, and a wide variety of publications, including *Writers News*. She is a member of the SWWJ and the Women Writers' Network. Carole Baldock is also author of *Writing Reviews*.

144pp. illus. 1 85703 244 6.

WRITING FOR TELEVISION
How to create and sell successful TV scripts

William Smethurst

Packed with hard-hitting information and advice, this is a complete step-by-step manual for every writer wanting to break into this lucrative market. 'He writes with such enthusiasm that he makes writing for TV seem like an exciting and fulfilling activity...I can state categorically that Mr Smethurst's advice does work.' *Writer's Monthly*. William Smethurst has written numerous scripts for both radio and television, has been a television script editor at BBC Pebble Mill, and executive producer of drama serials for Central Television. He is now a director of the independent television company, Andromeda Television Ltd.

156pp. illus. 1 85703 273 X. 2nd edition.